Collins gem

Collins Spanish phrasebook

Consultant
Lydia Batanaz

First published 1993
This edition published 2007

Reprint 10 9 8 7 6 5 4 3 2
Typeset by Davidson Pre-Press, Glasgow
Printed in Malaysia by Imago

www.collinslanguage.com

ISBN 978-0-00-724674-8

Using your phrasebook

Your *Collins Gem Phrasebook* is designed to help you locate the exact phrase you need, when you need it, whether on holiday or for business. If you want to adapt the phrases, you can easily see where to substitute your own words using the dictionary section, and the clear, full-colour layout gives you direct access to the different topics.

The Gem Phrasebook includes:

- Over 70 topics arranged thematically. Each phrase is accompanied by a simple pronunciation guide which eliminates any problems pronouncing foreign words.

- A Top ten tips section to safeguard against any cultural faux pas, giving essential dos and don'ts for situations involving local customs or etiquette.

- Practical hints to make your stay trouble free, showing you where to go and what to do when dealing with everyday matters such as travel or hotels and offering valuable tourist information.

- Face to face sections so that you understand what it is being said to you. These example mini-dialogues give you a good idea of what to expect from a real conversation.

- Common announcements and messages you may hear, ensuring that you never miss the important information you need to know when out and about.

- A clearly laid-out 3000-word dictionary means you will never be stuck for words.

- A basic grammar section which will enable you to build on your phrases.

- A list of public holidays to avoid being caught out by unexpected opening and closing hours, and to make sure you don't miss the celebrations!

It's worth spending time before you embark on your travels just looking through the topics to see what is covered and becoming familiar with what might be said to you.

Whatever the situation, your *Gem Phrasebook* is sure to help!

Contents

Pronouncing Spanish

Spelling and pronouncing Spanish are easy once you know the few basic rules. This book has been designed so that as you read the pronunciation of the phrases you can follow the Spanish. This will help you to recognize the different sounds and give you a feeling for the rhythm of the language. The syllable to be stressed is marked in **bold** in the pronunciation. Here are a few rules you should know:

Spanish	sounds like	example	pronunciation
ca	ka	cama	**ka**-ma
co	ko	con	kon
cu	ku	cubo	**koo**bo
ce	the	cena	**the**-na
ci	thee	cine	**thee**ne
ga	ga	gato	**ga**-to
go	go	algo	**al**go
gu	goo	algún	al**goon**
ge	khe	gente	**khen**te
gi	khee	giro	**khee**ro
j	kh	jueves	**khwe**-bes
ll	ly	llamo	**lya**-mo
ñ	ny	señor	se-**nyor**
ua	wa	cual	kwal

Spanish	sounds like	example	pronunciation
ue	**we**	**vuelva**	**bwel**ba
v	**b**	**vuelva**	**bwel**ba
z	**th**	**Zaragoza**	tha-ra-**go**-tha

h is silent: **hora o**-ra, **hola o**-la.
r is rolled and **rr** even more so.

In Spanish, vowels (**a**, **e**, **i**, **o**, **u**) have only one sound. When you find two together, pronounce both of them in quick succession, as in **aceite** a-**they**-te.

Top ten tips

1. Greet people with a '**Buenos días**' or '**Buenas tardes**' on entering a lift, as it's rude not to acknowledge them.

2. Spain is not a queuing country: people do not queue in bus stops. In places such as shops, banks, markets etc, people ask '**¿quién es el último?**' which means 'who is the last one?'

3. When addressing elders or people you have been just introduced to, use the formal '**Usted**' mode of address.

4. It is normal for people to stand or sit very close to each other when talking, which may be closer than you're used to. Pulling away from your counterpart may be regarded as unfriendly.

5. Taking up spare seats at a table that's already occupied is not common.

6. The Spanish do not make a habit of saying 'please' and 'thank you' very much – it is implied in the tone of voice. It is a cultural thing, so don't think they are being rude!

7 When you enter a restaurant or a home where people are eating, it's polite to say '**que aproveche**', meaning 'enjoy your meal'.

8 If you receive a gift, you should open it straightaway and in front of the giver.

9 Expect to be interrupted when speaking!

10 Cover your shoulders and legs when visiting religious buildings.

Talking to people

Hello/goodbye, yes/no

The word for Mr is **Señor** (se-**nyor**) and for Mrs/Ms **Señora** (se-**nyo**-ra).

Yes	**Sí** see
No	**No** no
OK!	**¡Vale!** ¡**ba**-le!
Thank you	**Gracias** **gra**-thyas
Thanks very much	**Muchas gracias** **moo**chas **gra**-thyas
Hello	**Hola** **o**-la
Goodbye	**Adiós** a-**dyos**
Good night	**Buenas noches** **bwe**-nas **no**-ches

Good morning	**Buenos días** **bwe**-nos **dee**-as
Good evening	**Buenas tardes** **bwe**-nas **tar**des
See you later	**Hasta luego** **as**ta **lwe**-go
Please	**Por favor** por fa-**bor**
Don't mention it	**De nada** de **na**-da
With pleasure!	**¡Con mucho gusto!** ¡kon **moo**cho **goos**to!
Pardon?	**¿Cómo dice?** ¿**ko**-mo **dee**the?
I'm sorry	**Lo siento** lo **syen**to
I don't know	**No sé** no se
Sir/Mr	**Señor/Sr.** se-**nyor**
Madam/Mrs/Ms	**Señora/Sra.** se-**nyo**-ra
Miss	**Señorita/Srta.** se-nyo-**ree**-ta
Excuse me! (to catch attention)	**¡Oiga, por favor!** ¡**oy**ga, por fa-**bor**!
Excuse me (sorry)	**Perdone** pair-**do**-ne

I don't understand	**No entiendo** no en-**tyen**-do
Do you understand?	**¿Entiende?** ¿en-**tyen**-de?
Do you speak English?	**¿Habla usted inglés?** ¿**a**-bla oos**ted** een**gles**?
I speak very little Spanish	**Hablo muy poco español** **a**-blo mwee **po**-ko es-pa-**nyol**
How are you?	**¿Cómo está?** ¿**ko**-mo es**ta**?
Fine, thanks	**Muy bien, gracias** mwee byen, **gra**-thyas
And you?	**¿Y usted?** ¿ee oos**ted**?

Key phrases

Asking for something in a shop or bar, you would ask for what you want, adding **por favor**.

the	**el/la/los/las** el/la/los/las
the museum	**el museo** el moo-**se**-o
the station	**la estación** la es-ta-**thyon**

the shops	**las tiendas** las **tyen**das
a/one (masc/fem)	**un/una** oon/**oo**na
a ticket	**un billete** oon bee-**lye**-te
one stamp	**un sello** oon **se**-lyo
a room	**una habitación** **oo**na a-bee-ta-**thyon**
one bottle	**una botella** **oo**na bo-**te**-lya
some (masculine)	**algún/alguno/algunos** al**goon**/al-**goo**-no/al-**goo**-nos
(feminine)	**alguna/algunas** al-**goo**-na/al-**goo**-nas
Would you like some bread?	**¿Quiere pan?** ¿**kye**-re pan?
Have you got some coffee?	**¿Tiene café?** ¿**tye**-ne ka-**fe**?
Do you have...?	**¿Tiene...?** ¿**tye**-ne...?
Do you have a room?	**¿Tiene una habitación?** ¿**tye**-ne **oo**na a-bee-ta-**thyon**?
I'd like...	**Querría...** ke-**rree**-a...
We'd like...	**Querríamos...** ke-**rree**-a-mos...

I'd like an ice cream	**Querría un helado** ke-**rree**-a oon e-**la**-do
We'd like to visit Toledo	**Querríamos visitar Toledo** ke-**rree**-a-mos bee-see-**tar** to-**le**-do
Some more bread?	**¿Más pan?** ¿mas pan?
Some more soup?	**¿Más sopa?** ¿mas **so**-pa?
Some more glasses?	**¿Más vasos?** ¿mas **ba**-sos?
Another coffee	**Otro café** **o**-tro ka-**fe**
Another beer	**Otra cerveza** **o**-tra thair-**be**-tha
How much is it?	**¿Cuánto es?** ¿**kwan**to es?
How much is the room?	**¿Cuánto cuesta la habitación?** ¿**kwan**to **kwes**ta la a-bee-ta-**thyon**?
large/small	**grande/pequeño** **gran**de/pe-**ke**-nyo
with/without	**con/sin** kon/seen
Where is...?	**¿Dónde está...?** ¿**don**de es**ta**...?
Where are...?	**¿Dónde están...?** ¿**don**de es**tan**...?

Where is the station?	**¿Dónde está la estación?** ¿**don**de es**ta** la es-ta-**thyon**?
Where are the toilets?	**¿Dónde están los aseos?** ¿**don**de es**tan** los a-**se**-os?
How do I get...?	**¿Cómo se va...?** ¿**ko**-mo se ba...?
to the park	**al parque** al **par**ke
to the station	**a la estación** a la es-ta-**thyon**
to Madrid	**a Madrid** a ma-**dreed**
There is/are...	**Hay...** **a**ee...
There isn't/ aren't any...	**No hay...** no **a**ee...
When...?	**¿Cuándo...?** ¿**kwan**do...?
At what time...?	**¿A qué hora...?** ¿a ke **o**-ra...?
today	**hoy** oy
tomorrow	**mañana** ma-**nya**-na
Can I smoke?	**¿Puedo fumar?** ¿**pwe**-do foo**mar**?
Can I taste it?	**¿Puedo probarlo?** ¿**pwe**-do pro-**bar**-lo?

How does this work? | **¿Cómo funciona?** ¿**ko**-mo foon-**thyo**-na?
What does this mean? | **¿Qué significa?** ¿ke seeg-nee-**fee**-ka?

How does this work?	**¿Cómo funciona?** ¿**ko**-mo foon-**thyo**-na?
What does this mean?	**¿Qué significa?** ¿ke seeg-nee-**fee**-ka?

Signs and notices

entrada	entrance
abierto	open
agua potable	drinking water
importe exacto	exact amount
no se admiten devoluciones	no refunds
no devuelve cambio	no change given
probadores	changing rooms
prohibido bañarse	no bathing
salida	exit
cerrado	closed
caliente	hot
frío	cold
caja	cash desk
autoservicio	self-service
tirar	pull
empujar	push
aseos	toilets
libre	vacant

ocupado	engaged
caballeros	gents
señoras	ladies
fuera de servicio	out of service
se aquila	for hire/to rent
se vende	for sale
rebajas	sale
sótano	basement
planta baja	ground floor
ascensor	lift
acceso a vías	to the trains
habitaciones libres	rooms available
salida de emergencia	emergency exit
completo	no vacancies
seleccione	choose
mañanas	mornings
tardes	afternoons
horario	timetable
llamar	ring
pulsar	press
billetes	tickets
salidas	departures
llegadas	arrivals
información	information
privado	private
no fumador	non-smoking
fumador	smoking
prohibido fumar	no smoking

Polite expressions

There are two forms of address in Spanish: formal (**usted**) and informal (**tú**). You should always stick to the formal until you are invited to **tutear** (use the informal **tú**).

The meal/dinner was delicious	**La comida/cena estaba deliciosa** la ko-**mee**-da/**the**-na es-**ta**-ba de-lee-**thyo**-sa
This is a gift for you	**Esto es un regalo para ti/vosotros** **es**to es oon re-**ga**-lo pa-ra tee/ bo-**so**-tros
Thank you very much	**Muchas gracias** **moo**chas **gra**-thyas
Pleased to meet you	**Encantado(a)** en-kan-**ta**-do(a)
This is...	**Le presento a...** le pre-**sen**-to a...
my husband/wife	**mi marido/mujer** mee ma-**ree**-do/moo**khair**
Enjoy your holiday!	**¡Que disfrute(n) de sus vacaciones!** ike dees-**froo**-te(n) de soos ba-ka-**thyo**-nes!

Celebrations

Traditional Christmas celebrations mainly take place on the night of **Nochebuena**, Christmas Eve. Presents are traditionally given on **los Reyes** or **el Día de Reyes** (6th January) but due to ever-increasing foreign influence some people also give presents on Christmas Day.

I'd like to wish you a...	**Le(Te) deseo que pase(s) un/unas...** le(te) de-**se**-o ke **pa**-se(s) oon/**oo**nas...
Happy Easter! / Merry Christmas!	**¡Felices Pascuas!/ ¡Feliz Navidad!** ife-**lee**-thes **pas**kwas!/ ife**leeth** na-bee-**dad**!
Happy New Year!	**¡Feliz Año (Nuevo)!** ife**leeth a**-nyo (**nwe**-bo)!
Happy birthday!	**¡Feliz cumpleaños!/ ¡Felicidades!** ife**leeth** koom-ple-**a**-nyos!/ ife-lee-thee-**da**-des!
Have a good trip!	**¡Buen viaje!** ibwen **bya**-khe!
Enjoy your meal!	**¡Que aproveche!** ike a-pro-**be**-che!

Making friends

In this section we have used the informal **tú** for the questions.

FACE TO FACE	
A	**¿Cómo te llamas?** ¿**ko**-mo te **lya**-mas? What's your name?
B	**Me llamo...** me **lya**-mo... My name is...
A	**¿De dónde eres?** ¿de **don**de **e**-res? Where are you from?
B	**Soy escocés(a), de Glasgow** soy es-ko-**the**-s(a), de **glas**gow I'm Scottish, from Glasgow **Encantado(a) de conocerte(le)** en-kan-**ta**-do(a) de ko-no-**thair**-te(le) Pleased to meet you

How old are you?	**¿Cuántos años tienes?** ¿**kwan**tos **a**-nyos **tye**-nes?
I'm ... years old	**Tengo ... años** **ten**go ... **a**-nyos
Where do you live?	**¿Dónde vives?** ¿**don**de **bee**bes?

Where do you live? (plural)	**¿Dónde vivís?** ¿**don**de bee**bees**?
I live in London	**Vivo en Londres** ¿**bee**bo en **lon**dres?
We live in Glasgow	**Vivimos en Glasgow** bee-**bee**-mos en **glas**gow
I'm still studying	**Todavía estoy estudiando** toda-**bee**-a es**toy** es-too-**dyan**-do
I work	**Trabajo** tra-**ba**-kho
I'm retired	**Estoy jubilado(a)** es**toy** khoo-bee-**la**-do(a)
I'm...	**Estoy...** es**toy**...
single	**soltero(a)** sol-**te**-ro(a)
married	**casado(a)** ka-**sa**-do(a)
divorced	**divorciado(a)** dee-bor-**thya**-do(a)
I have...	**Tengo...** **ten**go...
a boyfriend	**novio** **no**-byo
a girlfriend	**novia** **no**-bya
a partner	**pareja** pa-**re**-kha

I have ... children	**Tengo ... hijos** **ten**go ... **ee**khos
I have no children	**No tengo hijos** no **ten**go **ee**khos
I'm here...	**Estoy aquí...** es**toy** a-**kee**...
on holiday	**de vacaciones** de ba-ka-**thyo**-nes
for work	**por razones de trabajo** por ra-**tho**-nes de tra-**ba**-kho

Work

What work do you do?	**¿En qué trabaja?** ¿en ke tra-**ba**-kha?
Do you enjoy it?	**¿Le gusta?** ¿le **goo**sta?
I'm...	**Soy...** soy...
a doctor	**médico(a)** **me**-dee-ko(a)
a teacher	**profesor(a)** pro-fe-**sor**(a)
a secretary	**secretaria** se-kre-**ta**-rya
I'm self-employed	**Trabajo por cuenta propia** tra-**ba**-kho por **kwen**ta **pro**-pya

Weather

los chubascos los choo-**bas**-kos	showers
despejado des-pe-**kha**-do	clear
la lluvia la **lyoo**bya	rain
la niebla la **nye**-bla	fog
nublado noo-**bla**-do	cloudy

It's sunny	**Hace sol** **a**-the sol
It's raining	**Está lloviendo** es**ta** lyo-**byen**-do
It's snowing	**Está nevando** es**ta** ne-**ban**-do
It's windy	**Hace viento** **a**-the **byen**to
What a lovely day!	**¡Qué día más bueno!** ¡ke **dee**-a mas **bwe**-no!
What awful weather!	**¡Qué tiempo tan malo!** ¡ke **tyem**po tan **ma**-lo!
What will the weather be like tomorrow?	**¿Qué tiempo hará mañana?** ¿ke **tyem**po a-**ra** ma-**nya**-na?
Do you think it's going to rain?	**¿Cree que va a llover?** ¿**kre**-e ke ba a lyo-**bair**?

It's very hot	**Hace mucho calor** **a**-the **moo**cho ka-**lor**
Do you think there will be a storm?	**¿Cree que va a haber tormenta?** ¿**kre**-e ke ba a a-**bair** tor-**men**-ta?
Do you think it will snow?	**¿Le parece que va a nevar?** ¿le pa-**re**-the ke ba a ne-**bar**?
What is the temperature?	**¿Qué temperatura hace?** ¿ke tem-pe-ra-**too**-ra **a**-the?

Getting around

Asking the way

enfrente (de) en-**fren**-te (de)	opposite (to)
al lado de al **la**-do de	next to
cerca de **thair**ka de	near to
el semáforo el se-**ma**-fo-ro	traffic lights
en la esquina en la es-**kee**-na	at the corner

FACE TO FACE

A **Oiga, señor/señora, ¿cómo se va a la estación?**
¿**oy**ga, se-**nyor**/se-**nyo**-ra, **ko**-mo se ba a la es-ta-**thyon**?
Excuse me, how do I get to the station?

B **Siga recto, después de la iglesia gire a la derecha/izquierda**
seega **rek**to, des**pwes** de la ee-**gle**-sya **khee**re a la de-**re**-cha/eeth-**kyair**-da
Keep straight on, after the church turn right/left

A **¿Está lejos?**
¿es**ta** **le**-khos?
Is it far?

B **No, a doscientos metros/cinco minutos**
no, a dos-**thyen**-tos **me**-tros/**theen**ko mee-**noo**-tos
No, 200 metres/five minutes

A **Gracias!**
gra-thyas!
Thank you!

B **De nada**
de **na**-da
You're welcome

We're looking for...	**Estamos buscando...** es-**ta**-mos boos-**kan**-do...
Is it far?	**¿Está lejos?** ¿es**ta** **le**-khos?
Can I/we walk there?	**¿Se puede ir andando?** ¿se **pwe**-de eer an-**dan**-do?
How do I/we get to the centre of (name of town)?	**¿Cómo se va al centro de...?** ¿**ko**-mo se ba al **then**tro de...?
We're lost	**Nos hemos perdido** nos **e**-mos pair-**dee**-do
Can you show me where it is on the map?	**¿Puede indicarme dónde está en el mapa?** ¿**pwe**-de een-dee-**kar**-me **don**de es**ta** en el **ma**-pa?

YOU MAY HEAR...	
Después de pasar el puente des**pwes** de pa-**sar** el **pwen**te	After passing the bridge
Gire a la izquierda/ derecha **khee**re a la eeth-**kyair**-da/ de-**re**-cha	Turn left/right
Siga todo recto hasta llegar a... **see**ga **to**-do **rek**to **as**ta lye-**gar** a...	Keep straight on until you get to...

Bus and coach

A **bonobús** card is usually valid for 10 journeys and must be stamped on board the bus. The word for coach is **el autocar**.

FACE TO FACE	
A	**Oiga, ¿qué autobús va al centro?** **oy**ga, ¿ke ow-to-**boos** ba al **then**tro? Excuse me, which bus goes to the centre?
B	**El número quince** el **noo**-me-ro **keen**the Number fifteen

A **¿Dónde está la parada?**
¿**don**de es**ta** la pa-**ra**-da?
Where is the bus stop?

B **Allí, a la derecha**
a-**lyee,** a la de-**re**-cha
There, on the right

A **¿Dónde puedo comprar un bonobús?**
¿**don**de **pwe**-do kom**prar** un bo-no-**boos**?
Where can I buy a bonobus card?

B **En el kiosko**
en el kee-**os**-ko
At the news-stand

Is there a bus to...?	**¿Hay algún autobús que vaya a...?** ¿**a**ee al**goon** ow-to-**boos** ke **ba**-ya a...?
Where do I catch the bus to...?	**¿Dónde se coge el autobús para...?** ¿**don**de se **ko**-khe el ow-to-**boos** pa-ra...?
We're going to...	**Vamos a...** **ba**-mos a...
to the centre	**al centro** al **then**tro
to the beach	**a la playa** a la **pla**-ya

to the airport	**al aeropuerto**	al a-e-ro-**pwair**-to
to Toledo	**a Toledo**	a to-**le**-do
How often are the buses to...?	**¿Cada cuánto hay autobuses a...?**	¿**ka**-da **kwan**to **a**ee ow-to-**boo**-ses a...?
When is the first/the last bus to...?	**¿Cuándo sale el primer/ el último autobús para...?**	¿**kwan**do **sa**-le el pree**mair**/el **ool**-tee-mo ow-to-**boos** pa-ra...?
Please tell me when to get off	**Por favor, ¿me dice cuándo tengo que bajarme?**	por fa-**bor**, ¿me **dee**the **kwan**do **ten**go ke ba-**khar**-me?
Please let me off	**¿Me deja salir, por favor?**	¿me **de**-kha sa-**leer** por fa-**bor**?
This is my stop	**Me bajo en esta parada**	me **ba**-kho en **es**ta pa-**ra**-da

YOU MAY HEAR...	
Este autobús no para en... **es**te ow-to-**boos** no **pa**-ra en...	This bus doesn't stop in...
Tiene que coger el... **tye**-ne ke ko-**khair** el...	You have to catch the...

Metro

You can buy either **un metrobús**, which is valid for 10 journeys or **un abono de transporte**, which covers a month's travel on both bus and metro.

la entrada	la en-**tra**-da	entrance
la salida	la sa-**lee**-da	way out/exit
el andén	el an**den**	metro line

Where is the nearest metro station?	**¿Dónde está la estación de metro más cercana?** ¿**don**de es**ta** la es-ta-**thyon** de **me**-tro mas thair-**ka**-na?
I'm going to...	**Voy a...** boy a...
A metrobus ticket please	**Un metrobús, por favor** oon me-tro-**boos** por fa-**bor**
Do you have a map of the metro?	**¿Tiene un plano del metro?** ¿**tye**-ne oon **pla**-no del **me**-tro?
How do I/we get to...?	**¿Cómo se va a...?** ¿**ko**-mo se ba a...?
Do I have to change?	**¿Tengo que cambiar de línea?** ¿**ten**go ke kam**byar** de **lee**-ne-a?
What is the next stop?	**¿Cuál es la próxima parada?** ¿kwal es la **prok**-see-ma pa-**ra**-da?
Please let me through	**¿Me deja pasar, por favor?** ¿me **de**-kha pa-**sar**, por fa-**bor**?

> **Luggage** (p 94)

Train

There are three types of tickets on the high-speed AVE train – **Club**, **Preferente** and **Turista**. Prices vary according to time: **Punta** (peak), **Valle** (off-peak), and **Llano** (standard). A useful website is **www.renfe.es**

sencillo sen-**thee**-lyo	single/one-way
ida y vuelta **ee**da ee **bwel**ta	return
el horario el o-**ra**-ryo	timetable
salidas sa-**lee**-das	departures
llegadas lye-**ga**-das	arrivals
diario dee-**a**-ryo	daily

FACE TO FACE

A **¿A qué hora es el próximo tren para...?**
¿a ke **o**-ra es el **prok**-see-mo tren pa-ra...?
When is the next train to...?

B **A las cinco y diez**
a las **theen**ko ee dyeth
At 17.10

Querría tres billetes, por favor
ke-**rree**-a tres bee-**lye**-tes, por fa-**bor**
I'd like three tickets, please
¿sencillos o de ida y vuelta?
¿sen-**thee**-lyos o de **ee**da ee **bwel**ta?
single or return?

Where is the station?	**¿Dónde está la estación?** ¿**don**de es**ta** la es-ta-**thyon**?
Two return tickets to...	**Dos billetes de ida y vuelta a...** dos bee-**lye**-tes de **ee**da ee **bwel**ta a...
A single to...	**Un billete de ida a...** oon bee-**lye**-te de **ee**da a...
Tourist class	**De clase turista** de **kla**-se too-**rees**-ta
Is there a supplement to pay?	**¿Hay que pagar suplemento?** ¿**a**ee ke pa-**gar** soo-ple-**men**-to?
I want to book a seat on the AVE to Seville	**Querría reservar un asiento en el AVE a Sevilla** ke-**rree**-a re-sair-**bar** oon a-**syen**-to en el **a**-be a se-**bee**-lya
When is the first/ last train to...?	**¿Cuándo es el primer/último tren para...?** ¿**kwan**do es el pree**mair**/ el **ool**-tee-mo tren pa-ra...?

Do I have to change?	**¿Tengo que hacer transbordo?** ¿**ten**go ke a-**thair** trans-**bor**-do?
Where?	**¿Dónde?** ¿**don**de?
Which platform does it leave from?	**¿De qué andén sale?** ¿de ke an**den** **sa**-le?
Is this the right platform for the train to...?	**¿Sale de este andén el tren para...?** ¿**sa**-le de **es**te an**den** el tren pa-ra...?
Is this the train for...?	**¿Es este el tren para...?** ¿es **es**te el tren pa-ra...?
When will it leave?	**¿Cuándo saldrá?** ¿**kwan**do sal**dra**?
Does the train stop at...?	**¿Para el tren en...?** ¿**pa**-ra el tren en...?
When does it arrive in...?	**¿Cuándo llega a...?** ¿**kwan**do **lye**-ga a...?
Please let me know when we get to...	**Por favor, ¿me avisa cuando lleguemos a...?** por fa-**bor**, ¿me a-**bee**-sa **kwan**do lye-**ge**-mos a...?
Is there a buffet on the train?	**¿Hay servicio de cafetería en el tren?** ¿**a**ee sair-**bee**-thyo de ka-fe-te-**ree**-a en el tren?
Is this free? (seat)	**¿Está libre?** ¿es**ta** **lee**bre?
Excuse me	**¡Perdón!** ¡pair**don**!

Taxi

In most places taxis are plentiful, reliable and not very expensive. Prices may often be displayed at the taxi stand.

I need a taxi	**Necesito un taxi** ne-the-**see**-to oon **tak**see
Where is the taxi stand?	**¿Dónde está la parada de taxis?** ¿**don**de es**ta** la pa-**ra**-da de **tak**sees?
Please order me a taxi	**Por favor, ¿me pide un taxi?** por fa-**bor**, ¿me **pee**de oon **tak**see?
straightaway	**enseguida** en-se-**gee**-da
for (time)	**para las...** pa-ra las...
How much is the taxi fare...?	**¿Cuánto cuesta ir en taxi...?** ¿**kwan**to **kwes**ta eer en **tak**see...?
into town	**al centro** al **then**tro
to the hotel	**al hotel** al o-**tel**
to the station	**a la estación** a la es-ta-**thyon**
to the airport	**al aeropuerto** al a-e-ro-**pwair**-to

to this address	**a esta dirección** a **es**ta dee-rek-**thyon**
Please take me/ us to...	**Me/Nos lleva a ... por favor** me/nos **lye**-ba a ... por fa-**bor**
How much is it?	**¿Cuánto es?** ¿**kwan**to es?
Why are you charging me so much?	**¿Cómo me cobra tanto?** ¿**ko**-mo me **ko**-bra **tan**to?
It's more than on the meter	**Es más de lo que marca el taxímetro** es mas de lo ke **mar**ka el tak-**see**-me-tro
Keep the change	**Quédese con la vuelta** **ke**-de-se kon la **bwel**ta
Sorry, I don't have any change	**Lo siento, no tengo nada de cambio** lo **syen**to, no **ten**go **na**-da de **kam**byo
I'm in a hurry	**Tengo mucha prisa** **ten**go **moo**cha **pree**sa

Boat and ferry

la travesía	la tra-be-**see**-a	crossing
el crucero	el kroo-**the**-ro	cruise
el camarote	el ka-ma-**ro**-te	cabin

When is the next boat/ferry to...?	**¿Cuándo sale el próximo barco/ferry para...?** ¿**kwan**do **sa**-le el **prok**-see-mo **bar**ko/**fe**rry pa-ra...?
Have you a timetable?	**¿Tienen un horario?** ¿**tye**-nen oon o-**ra**-ryo?
Is there a car ferry to...?	**¿Hay ferry para coches a...?** ¿**a**ee **fe**rry pa-ra **ko**-ches a?
How much is a ticket...?	**¿Cuánto cuesta el billete...?** ¿**kwan**to **kwes**ta el bee-**lye**-te...?
single	**sencillo/de ida** sen-**thee**-lyo/de **ee**da
return	**de ida y vuelta** de **ee**da ee **bwel**ta
A tourist ticket	**Un billete de clase turista** oon bee-**lye**-te de **kla**-se too-**rees**-ta
How much is the crossing for a car and ... people?	**¿Cuánto cuesta un pasaje para ... personas y un coche?** ¿**kwan**to **kwes**ta oon pa-**sa**-khe pa-ra ... pair-**so**-nas ee oon **ko**-che?
How long is the journey?	**¿Cuánto dura el viaje?** ¿**kwan**to **doo**ra el **bya**-khe?
What time do we get to...?	**¿A qué hora llegamos a...?** ¿a ke **o**-ra lye-**ga**-mos a...?
Where does the boat leave from?	**¿De dónde sale el barco?** ¿de **don**de **sa**-le el **bar**ko?

When is the first/ the last boat?	**¿Cuándo sale el primer/ el último barco?** ¿**kwan**do **sa**-le el pree**mair**/ el **ool**-tee-mo **bar**ko?
Is there somewhere to eat on the boat?	**¿Hay cafetería/restaurante en el barco?** ¿**a**ee ka-fe-te-**ree**-a/res-tow-**ran**-te en el **bar**ko?

Air travel

How do I get to the airport?	**¿Cómo se va al aeropuerto?** ¿**ko**-mo se ba al a-e-ro-**pwair**-to?
To the airport, please	**Al aeropuerto, por favor** al a-e-ro-**pwair**-to, por fa-**bor**
I have to catch...	**Tengo que coger...** **ten**go ke kho-**khair**...
the ... o'clock flight to...	**el vuelo de las ... para...** el **bwe**-lo de las ... pa-ra...
Is there a bus to the airport?	**¿Hay algún autobús al aeropuerto?** ¿**a**ee al**goon** ow-to-**boos** al a-e-ro-**pwair**-to?
How do I/we get to the centre of (name of town)?	**¿Cómo se va al centro de...?** ¿**ko**-mo se ba al **then**tro de...?

Is there a bus to the city centre?	**¿Hay algún autobús que vaya al centro?** ¿**a**ee al**goon** ow-to-**boos** ke **ba**-ya al **then**tro?
Where is the luggage for the flight from...?	**¿Dónde está el equipaje del vuelo de...?** ¿**don**de es**ta** el e-kee-**pa**-khe del **bwe**-lo de...?

YOU MAY HEAR...	
El embarque se efectuará por la puerta número... el em-**bar**-ke se e-fek-twa-**ra** por la **pwair**ta **noo**-me-ro...	Boarding will take place at gate number...
Última llamada para los pasajeros del vuelo... **ool**-tee-ma lya-**ma**-da pa-ra los pa-sa-**khe**-ros del **bwe**-lo...	Last call for passengers on flight number...
Su vuelo sale con retraso soo **bwe**-lo **sa**-le kon re-**tra**-so	Your flight is delayed

Customs control

With the single European Market, European Union (EU) citizens are subject only to highly selective spot checks and they can go through the blue customs channel when arriving from another EU country.

UE oo eh	EU
la aduana la a-doo-**a**-na	customs control
el pasaporte el pa-sa-**por**-te	passport

Do I have to pay duty on this?	**¿Tengo que pagar derechos de aduana por esto?** ¿**ten**go ke pa**gar** de-**re**-chos de a-doo-**a**-na por **es**to?
It is for my own personal use	**Es para uso personal** es pa-ra **oo**so pair-so-**nal**
We are on our way to... (if in transit through a country)	**Estamos aquí de paso. Vamos a...** es-**ta**-mos a-**kee** de **pa**-so. **ba**-mos a...

Driving

Car hire

el permiso de conducir el pair-**mee**-so de kon-doo-**theer**	driving licence
el seguro el se-**goo**-ro	insurance
la marcha atrás la **mar**cha a-**tras**	reverse gear

I want to hire a car	**Querría alquilar un coche** ke-**rree**-a al-kee-**lar** oon **ko**-che
for ... days/the weekend	**para ... días/el fin de semana** pa-ra ... **dee**as/el feen de se-**ma**-na
What are your rates...?	**¿Qué tarifas tienen...?** ¿ke ta-**ree**-fas **tye**-nen...?
per day	**por día** por **dee**a
per week	**por semana** por se-**ma**-na
How much is the deposit?	**¿Cuánto hay que dejar de depósito?** ¿**kwan**to **a**ee ke de-**khar** de de-**po**-see-to?

Is there a mileage (km) charge?	**¿Hay que pagar kilometraje?** ¿**a**ee ke pa-**gar** kee-lo-me-**tra**-khe?
How much?	**¿Cuánto?** ¿**kwan**to?
Is fully comprehensive insurance included in the price?	**¿El seguro a todo riesgo va incluido en el precio?** ¿el se-**goo**-ro a **to**-do **ryes**go ba een-kloo-**ee**-do en el **pre**-thyo?
Do I have to return the car here?	**¿Tengo que devolver el coche aquí mismo?** ¿**ten**go ke de-bol-**bair** el **ko**-che a-**kee mees**mo?
By what time?	**¿Para qué hora?** ¿pa-ra ke **o**-ra?
I'd like to leave it in...	**Quisiera dejarlo en...** kee-**sye**-ra de-**khar**-lo en...
Can you show me how the controls work?	**¿Me enseña cómo funcionan los mandos?** ¿me en-**se**-nya **ko**-mo foon-**thyo**-nan los **man**dos?

Driving

YOU MAY HEAR...	
Por favor, devuelva el coche con el depósito lleno por fa-**bor**, de-**bwel**ba el **ko**-che kon el de-**po**-see-to **lye**-no	Please return the car with a full tank

Driving

The speed limits in Spain are 50 km/h in built-up areas, 90 km/h on ordinary roads and 120 km/h on **autovías** (dual carriageways) and **autopistas** (motorways). Some motorways are toll paying (**peaje**). Payment is due on completion of each section. A useful website for motorway information is **www.aseta.es**

Can I/we park here?	**¿Se puede aparcar aquí?** ¿se **pwe**-de a-par-**kar** a-**kee**?
How long can I/we park for here?	**¿Cuánto tiempo se puede aparcar aquí?** ¿**kwan**to **tyem**po se **pwe**-de a-par-**kar** a-**kee**?
How do I/we get to the motorway?	**¿Por dónde se va a la autopista?** ¿por **don**de se ba a la ow-to-**pee**-sta?
Which junction is it for...?	**¿Cuál es la salida de...?** ¿kwal es la sa-**lee**-da de...?
Do I/we need snow chains?	**¿Hace falta usar cadenas?** ¿**a**-the **fal**ta oo**sar** ka-**de**-nas?

Driving

Petrol

Unleaded petrol pumps are always coloured green.

sin plomo seen **plo**-mo	unleaded
gasoil/gasóleo ga-**soyl**/ga-**so**-le-o	diesel
el surtidor el soor-tee-**dor**	petrol pump

Is there a petrol station near here?	**¿Hay una estación de servicio por aquí cerca?** ¿**a**ee **oo**na es-ta-**thyon** de sair-**bee**-thyo por a-**kee thair**ka?
Fill it up, please	**Lleno, por favor** **lye**-no, por fa-**bor**
Can you check the oil/the water?	**¿Me revisa el aceite/el agua?** ¿me re-**bee**-sa el a-**the**-ee-te/ el **a**-gwa?
...euros worth of unleaded petrol	**...euros de gasolina sin plomo** ...**eoo**-ros de ga-so-**lee**-na seen **plo**-mo
Where is...?	**¿Dónde está...?** ¿**don**de es**ta**...?
the air	**el aire** el **aee**-re
the water	**el agua** el **a**-gwa

Can you check the tyre pressure, please?	**¿Me revisa la presión de los neumáticos, por favor?** ¿me re-**bee**-sa la pre-**syon** de los neoo-**ma**-tee-kos, por fa-**bor**?
Can I pay with this credit card?	**¿Puedo pagar con esta tarjeta de crédito?** ¿**pwe**-do pa-**gar** kon **es**ta tar-**khe**-ta de **kre**-dee-to?

YOU MAY HEAR...

¿Qué surtidor ha usado? ¿ke soor-tee-**dor** a oo-**sa**-do?	Which pump did you use?

Breakdown

Can you help me?	**¿Puede ayudarme?** ¿**pwe**-de a-yoo-**dar**-me?
My car has broken down	**Se me ha averiado el coche** se me a a-be-**rya**-do el **ko**-che
I've run out of petrol	**Me he quedado sin gasolina** me e ke-**da**-do seen ga-so-**lee**-na
Is there a garage near here?	**¿Hay un taller por aquí cerca?** ¿**a**ee oon ta-**lyair** por a-**kee** **thair**ka?
I've got a flat tyre	**Tengo una rueda pinchada** **ten**go **oo**na **rwe**-da peen-**cha**-da

Do you have parts for a (make of car)?	**¿Tiene repuestos para el...?**	¿**tye**-ne re-**pwes**-tos pa-ra el...?
The ... doesn't work properly (see car parts)	**El/La ... no funciona bien**	el/la ... no foon-**thyo**-na byen
Can you replace ....?	**¿Me puede cambiar ....?**	¿me **pwe**-de kam**byar**?

Car parts

The ... doesn't work	**El/La ... no funciona**	el/la ... no foon-**thyo**-na
The ... don't work	**Los/Las ... no funcionan**	los/las ... no foon-**thyo**-nan

accelerator	**el acelerador**	a-the-le-ra-**dor**
battery	**la batería**	ba-te-**ree**-a
bonnet	**el capó**	ka-**po**
brakes	**los frenos**	**fre**-nos
choke	**el estárter**	es-**tar**-tair
clutch	**el embrague**	em-**bra**-ge
distributor	**el distribuidor**	dees-tree-bwee-**dor**
engine	**el motor**	mo-**tor**
exhaust pipe	**el tubo de escape**	**too**bo de es-**ka**-pe
fuse	**el fusible**	foo-**see**-ble

gears	**las marchas**	**mar**chas
handbrake	**el freno de mano**	**fre**-no de **ma**-no
headlights	**los faros**	**fa**-ros
ignition	**el encendido**	en-then-**dee**-do
indicator	**el intermitente**	een-tair-mee-**ten**-te
points	**los platinos**	pla-**tee**-nos
radiator	**el radiador**	ra-dya-**dor**
rear lights	**los pilotos**	pee-**lo**-tos
seat belt	**el cinturón de seguridad**	theen-too-**ron** de se-goo-ree-**dad**
spare wheel	**la rueda de repuesto**	**rwe**-da de re-**pwes**-to
spark plugs	**las bujías**	boo-**khee**-as
steering	**la dirección**	dee-rek-**thyon**
steering wheel	**el volante**	bo-**lan**-te
tyre	**el neumático**	neoo-**ma**-tee-ko
wheel	**la rueda**	**rwe**-da
windscreen	**el parabrisas**	pa-ra-**bree**-sas
windscreen washer	**el lavaparabrisas**	la-ba-pa-ra-**bree**-sas
windscreen wiper	**el limpiaparabrisas**	leem-pya-pa-ra-**bree**-sas

Car parts

Road signs

danger

dangerous bends

spaces

full

give way

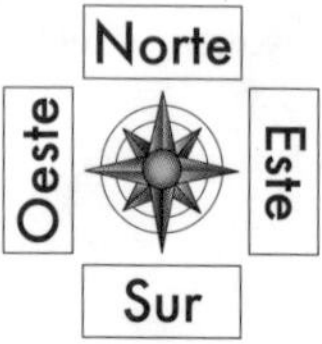

NO APARCAR

no parking

NO ESTACIONAR

no stopping

SENTIDO ÚNICO

one way

end of right of way

AUTOVÍA

dual carriageway

AUTOPISTA

motorway

Staying somewhere

Hotel (booking)

FACE TO FACE

A **Querría reservar una habitación individual/ doble**
ke-**rree**-a re-sair-**bar oo**na a-bee-ta-**thyon** een-dee-bee-**dwal**/**do**-ble
I'd like to book a single/double room

B **¿Para cuántas noches?**
¿pa-ra **kwan**tas **no**-ches?
For how many nights?

A **Para una noche/... noches ; del ... al ...**
pa-ra **oo**na **no**-che/... **no**-ches ; del ... al ...
For one night/... nights ; from ... till ...

Do you have a room for tonight?

¿Tiene una habitación para esta noche?
¿**tye**-ne **oo**na a-bee-ta-**thyon** pa-ra **es**ta **no**-che?

double	**doble**	
	do-ble	
single	**individual**	
	een-dee-bee-**dwal**	
with bath	**con baño**	
	kon **ba**nyo	
with shower	**con ducha**	
	kon **doo**cha	
with a double bed	**con cama de matrimonio**	
	kon **ka**-ma de ma-tree-**mo**-nyo	
twin-bedded	**con dos camas**	
	kon dos **ka**-mas	
How much is it...?	**¿Qué precio tiene...?**	
	¿ke **pre**-thyo **tye**-ne...?	
per night	**por noche**	
	por **no**-che	
per week	**por semana**	
	por se-**ma**-na	
for half board	**con media pensión**	
	kon **me**-dya pen**syon**	
full board	**con pensión completa**	
	kon pen**syon** kom-**ple**-ta	
with breakfast	**con desayuno**	
	kon de-sa-**yoo**-no	
Is breakfast included?	**¿Está incluido el desayuno?**	
	¿es**ta** een-kloo-**ee**-do el de-sa-**yoo**-no?	

Is there room service?	**¿Hay servicio de habitaciones?** ¿**a**ee sair-**bee**-thyo de a-bee-ta-**thyo**-nes?
Can I see the room?	**¿Puedo ver la habitación?** ¿**pwe**-do bair la a-bee-ta-**thyon**?

YOU MAY HEAR...	
Está todo ocupado es**ta to**-do o-koo-**pa**-do	We're full
¿Para cuántas noches? ¿pa-ra **kwan**tas **no**-ches?	For how many nights?
¿Su nombre, por favor? ¿soo **nom**bre, por fa-**bor**?	Your name, please?
Por favor confírmelo... por fa-**bor** kon-**feer**-me-lo...	Please confirm...
por escrito por es-**kree**-to	by letter
por fax por faks	by fax

Hotel desk

You may be required to fill in a registration form and give your passport number.

I booked a room...	**Tengo una habitación reservada...** **ten**go **oo**na a-bee-ta-**thyon** re-sair-**ba**-da...
in the name of...	**a nombre de...** a **nom**bre de...
Where can I park the car?	**¿Dónde puedo aparcar el coche?** ¿**don**de **pwe**-do a-par-**kar** el **ko**-che?
What time is...?	**¿A qué hora es...?** ¿a ke **o**-ra es...?
dinner	**la cena** la **the**-na
breakfast	**el desayuno** el de-sa-**yoo**-no
The key for room number...	**¿Me da la llave de la habitación...?** ¿me da la **lya**-be de la a-bee-ta-**thyon**...?
I'm leaving tomorrow	**Me voy mañana** me boy ma-**nya**-na
Please prepare the bill	**¿Me prepara la cuenta, por favor?** ¿me pre-**pa**-ra la **kwen**ta, por fa-**bor**?

Camping

Local tourist offices should have **una guía de campings** with prices.

How far is the beach?	**¿A qué distancia está la playa?** ¿a ke dees-**tan**-thya es**ta** la **pla**-ya?
Is there a restaurant on the campsite?	**¿Hay restaurante en el camping?** ¿**a**ee res-tow-**ran**-te en el **kam**peen?
Do you have any vacancies?	**¿Tienen plazas libres?** ¿**tye**-nen **pla**-thas **lee**bres?
Is hot water included in the price?	**¿El agua caliente va incluida en el precio?** ¿el **a**-gwa ka-**lyen**-te ba een-kloo-**ee**-da en el **pre**-thyo?
We'd like to stay for ... nights	**Quisiéramos quedarnos... noches** kee-**sye**-ra-mos ke-**dar**-nos ... **no**-ches
How much is it per night...?	**¿Cuánto cuesta por noche...?** ¿**kwan**to **kwes**ta por **no**-che...?
for a tent	**por tienda** por **tyen**da
per person	**por persona** por pair-**so**-na

Self-catering

If you arrive with no accommodation and want to go self-catering, look for signs **Alquiler de Apartamentos** (apartments for rent).

Who do we contact if there are problems?	**¿A quién avisamos si hay algún problema?** ¿a kyen a-bee-**sa**-mos see **a**ee al**goon** pro-**ble**-ma?
How does the heating work?	**¿Cómo funciona la calefacción?** ¿**ko**-mo foon-**thyo**-na la ka-le-fak-**thyon**?
Where is the nearest supermarket?	**¿Dónde está el supermercado más cercano?** ¿**don**de es**ta** el soo-pair-mair-**ka**-do mas thair-**ka**-no?
Where do we leave the rubbish?	**¿Dónde se deja la basura?** ¿**don**de se **de**-kha la ba-**soo**-ra?

> **Sightseeing and tourist office** (p 69)

Shopping

Shopping phrases

Most shops close for lunch approx. 1.30 to 5.00 or 5.30 pm and stay open till about 8.30 pm. Department stores remain open all day.

YOU MAY HEAR...	
¿Qué desea? ¿ke de-**se**-a?	Can I help you?
¿Tiene...? ¿**tye**-ne...?	Do you have...?
Por supuesto, aquí tiene por soo-**pwes**-to, a-**kee** **tye**-ne	Certainly, here you are
¿Algo más? ¿**al**go mas?	Anything else?

Where is...? **¿Dónde está...?**
¿**don**de es**ta**?

Where can I buy...? **¿Dónde puedo comprar...?**
¿**don**de **pwe**-do kom**prar**...?

Shopping

toys	**juguetes** khoo-**ge**-tes
gifts	**regalos** re-**ga**-los
I'm looking for a present for...	**Estoy buscando un regalo para...** es**toy** boos-**kan**-do oon re-**ga**-lo pa-ra...
my mother	**mi madre** mee **ma**-dre
a child	**un niño** oon **neen**yo
Which floor are shoes on?	**¿En qué planta están los zapatos?** ¿en ke **plan**ta es**tan** los tha-**pa**-tos?
Where is the lingerie department?	**¿Dónde está la sección de lencería?** ¿**don**de es**ta** la sek**thyon** de len-the-**ree**-a?
It's too expensive for me	**Me resulta demasiado caro** me re-**sool**-ta de-ma-**sya**-do **ka**-ro
Have you anything else?	**¿No tiene otra cosa?** ¿no **tye**-ne **o**-tra **ko**-sa?

Shops

liquidación/rebajas lee-kee-da-**thyon/** re-**ba**-khas	sale/reductions
hoy abierto hasta las... hoy a-**byair**-to **as**ta las...	open today till...

baker's	**panadería**	pa-na-de-**ree**-a
butcher's	**carnicería**	kar-nee-the-**ree**-a
cake shop	**pastelería/ confitería**	pas-te-le-**ree**-a/ kon-fee-te-**ree**-a
clothes (women's)	**ropa de señora**	**ro**-pa de se-**nyo**-ra
clothes (men's)	**ropa de caballero**	**ro**-pa de ka-ba-**lye**-ro
clothes (children's)	**ropa de niños**	**ro**-pa de **neen**yos
fishmonger's	**pescadería**	pes-ka-de-**ree**-a
gifts	**regalos**	re-**ga**-los
greengrocer's	**frutería**	froo-te-**ree**-a
grocer's	**tienda de comestibles**	**tyen**da de ko-mes-**tee**-bles
hairdresser's	**peluquería**	pe-loo-ke-**ree**-a
jeweller's	**joyería**	kho-ye-**ree**-a
pharmacy	**farmacia**	far-**ma**-thya
shoe shop	**zapatería**	tha-pa-te-**ree**-a
sports	**deportes**	de-**por**-tes

supermarket	**supermercado**	soo-pair-mair-**ka**-do
tobacconist's	**estanco**	es-**tan**-ko
toys	**juguetes**	khoo-**ge**-tes

Food (general)

biscuits	**las galletas**	ga-**lye**-tas
bread	**el pan**	pan
bread (wholemeal)	**el pan integral**	pan een-te-**gral**
bread roll	**el panecillo**	pa-ne-**thee**-lyo
butter	**la mantequilla**	man-te-**kee**-lya
cereal	**los cereales**	the-re-**a**-les
cheese	**el queso**	**ke**-so
chicken	**el pollo**	**po**-lyo
coffee (instant)	**el café (instantáneo)**	ka-**fe** (eens-tan-**ta**-ne-o)
cream	**la nata**	**na**-ta
crisps	**las patatas fritas**	pa-**ta**-tas **free**-tas
eggs	**los huevos**	**we**-bos
flour	**la harina**	a-**ree**-na
ham (cooked)	**el jamón (de) York**	kha-**mon** (de) york
ham (cured)	**el jamón serrano**	kha-**mon** se-**rra**-no

Food (general)

herbal tea	**la infusión**	een-foo-**syon**
honey	**la miel**	myel
jam	**la mermelada**	mair-me-**la**-da
margarine	**la margarina**	mar-ga-**ree**-na
marmalade	**la mermelada de naranja**	mair-me-**la**-da de na-**ran**-kha
milk	**la leche**	**le**-che
mustard	**la mostaza**	mos-**ta**-tha
olive oil	**el aceite de oliva**	a-**they**-te de o-**lee**-ba
orange juice	**el zumo de naranja**	**thoo**mo de na-**ran**-kha
pepper	**la pimienta**	pee-**myen**-ta
rice	**el arroz**	a-**rroth**
salt	**la sal**	sal
stock cube	**el cubito de caldo**	koo-**bee**-to de **kal**do
sugar	**el azúcar**	a-**thoo**-kar
tea	**el té**	te
tin of tomatoes	**la lata de tomate**	**la**-ta de to-**ma**-te
vinegar	**el vinagre**	bee-**na**-gre
yoghurt	**el yogur**	yo-**goor**

Shopping

> **Measurements and quantities** (p 115)

Food (fruit and veg)

Fruit

apples	**las manzanas**	man-**tha**-nas
apricots	**los albaricoques**	al-ba-ree-**ko**-kes
bananas	**los plátanos**	**pla**-ta-nos
cherries	**las cerezas**	the-**re**-thas
grapefruit	**el pomelo**	po-**me**-lo
grapes	**las uvas**	**oo**bas
lemon	**el limón**	lee**mon**
melon	**el melón**	me-**lon**
nectarines	**las nectarinas**	nek-ta-**ree**-nas
oranges	**las naranjas**	na-**ran**-khas
peaches	**los melocotones**	me-lo-ko-**to**-nes
pears	**las peras**	**pe**-ras
pineapple	**la piña**	**pee**nya
plums	**las ciruelas**	thee-**rwe**-las
raspberries	**las frambuesas**	fram-**bwe**-sas
strawberries	**las fresas**	**fre**-sas
watermelon	**la sandía**	san-**dee**-a

Vegetables

asparagus	**los espárragos**	es-**pa**-rra-gos
carrots	**las zanahorias**	tha-na-**o**-ryas

cauliflower	**la coliflor**	ko-lee-**flor**
courgettes	**los calabacines**	ka-la-ba-**thee**-nes
French beans	**las judías verdes**	khoo-**dee**-as **bair**des
garlic	**el ajo**	**a**-kho
leeks	**los puerros**	**pwe**rros
lettuce	**la lechuga**	le-**choo**ga
mushrooms	**los champiñones**	cham-pee-**nyo**-nes
onions	**las cebollas**	the-**bo**-lyas
peas	**los guisantes**	gee-**san**-tes
peppers	**los pimientos**	pee-**myen**-tos
potatoes	**las patatas**	pa-**ta**-tas
spinach	**las espinacas**	es-pee-**na**-kas
tomatoes	**los tomates**	to-**ma**-tes

Clothes

women's sizes		men's suit sizes		shoe sizes			
UK	EU	UK	EU	UK	EU	UK	EU
8	36	36	46	2	35	7	41
10	38	38	48	3	36	8	42
12	40	40	50	4	37	9	43
14	42	42	52	5	38	10	44
16	44	44	54	6	39	11	45
18	46	46	56				

FACE TO FACE

¿Puedo probarmelo?
¿**pwe**-do pro-**bar**-me-lo?
May I try this on?

Sí, los probadores están allí
see, los pro-ba-**do**-res es**tan** a-**lyee**
Yes, the changing rooms are over there

¿Tiene una talla pequeña/mediana/grande/ extra grande?
¿**tye**-ne **oo**na **ta**-lya pe-**ke**-nya/me-**dya**-na/ **gran**de/**eks**tra **gran**de?
Do you have a small/medium/large/extra large size?

Sólo tenemos esta talla en este color
so-lo te-**ne**-mos **es**ta **ta**-lya en **es**te co-**lor**
In this colour we only have this size

Where are the changing rooms?	**¿Dónde están los probadores?** ¿**don**de es**tan** los pro-ba-**do**-res?
I take size 42 (clothes)	**Uso la cuarenta y dos** **oo**so la kwa-**ren**-ta ee **dos**
I take size 39 (shoes)	**Uso el treinta y nueve** **oo**so el **treyn**ta ee **nwe**-be
I'd like to return...	**Quiero devolver...** **kye**-ro de-bol-**bair**...
Can I have my money back?	**¿Me devuelven el dinero?** ¿me de-**bwel**-ben el dee-**ne**-ro?

I'm just looking	**Solo estoy mirando** **so**-lo es**toy** mee-**ran**-do	
I'll take it	**Me lo llevo** me lo **lye**-vo	

Clothes (articles)

belt	**el cinturón**	theen-too-**ron**
blouse	**la blusa**	**bloo**sa
bra	**el sujetador**	soo-khe-ta-**dor**
coat	**el abrigo**	a-**bree**-go
dress	**el vestido**	bes-**tee**-do
gloves	**los guantes**	**gwan**tes
hat	**el sombrero**	som-**bre**-ro
hat (woollen)	**el gorro**	**go**-rro
jacket	**la chaqueta**	cha-**ke**-ta
jeans	**los vaqueros**	ba-**ke**-ros
knickers	**las bragas**	**bra**-gas
nightdress	**el camisón**	ka-mee-**son**
pyjamas	**el pijama**	pee-**kha**-ma
raincoat	**el chubasquero**	choo-bas-**ke**-ro
sandals	**las sandalias**	san-**da**-lyas
scarf (silk)	**el pañuelo**	pa-**nwe**-lo
scarf (wool)	**la bufanda**	boo-**fan**-da
shirt	**la camisa**	ka-**mee**-sa

> **Paying** (p 93) > **Numbers** (p 117)

shorts	**los pantalones cortos**	pan-ta-**lo**-nes **kor**tos
skirt	**la falda**	**fal**da
slippers	**las zapatillas**	tha-pa-**tee**-lyas
socks	**los calcetines**	kal-the-**tee**-nes
suit	**el traje**	**tra**-khe
swimsuit	**el traje de baño/ el bañador**	**tra**-khe de **ba**-nyo/ba-nya-**dor**
tie	**la corbata**	kor-**ba**-ta
tights	**las medias**	**me**-dyas
tracksuit	**el chándal**	**chan**-dal
trousers	**los pantalones**	pan-ta-**lo**-nes
t-shirt	**la camiseta**	ka-mee-**se**-ta
underpants	**los calzoncillos**	kal-thon-**thee**-lyos
zip	**la cremallera**	kre-ma-**lye**-ra

Maps and guides

Have you...?	**¿Tiene...?** ¿**tye**-ne...?
a map of (name of town)	**un plano de...** oon **pla**-no de...
a map of the region	**un mapa de la zona** oon **ma**-pa de la **tho**-na

Can you show me where ... is on the map?	**¿Puede indicarme en el mapa dónde está...?** ¿**pwe**-de een-dee-**kar**-me en el **ma**-pa **don**de es**ta**...?
Do you have a guide book/a leaflet in English?	**¿Tiene alguna guía/algún folleto en inglés?** ¿**tye**-ne al-**goo**-na **gee**-a/ al**goon** fo-**lye**-to en een**gles**?
Where can I/we buy an English newspaper/ magazine?	**¿Dónde se pueden comprar periódicos ingleses/revistas inglesas?** ¿**don**de se **pwe**-den kom**prar** pe-ree-**o**-dee-kos een-**gle**-ses/ re-**bis**-tas een-**gle**-sas?

Shopping

Post office

Generally open from 8.30 am to 8.30 pm Monday to Friday and from 9.30 am to 2 pm on Saturdays. Opening times can be checked at **www.correo.es**.

(la oficina de) correos (la o-fee-**thee**-na de) ko-**rre**-os	post office
el buzón el boo**thon**	postbox
los sellos los **se**-lyos	stamps

> **Asking the way** (p 26)

Is there a post office near here?	**¿Hay una oficina de Correos por aquí cerca?**	¿**a**ee oon o-fee-**thee**-na de ko-**rre**-os por a-**kee thair**ka?
Do you sell stamps?	**¿Venden sellos?**	¿**ben**den **se**-lyos?
Can I have stamps for ... postcards to Great Britain	**Me da sellos para ... postales para Gran Bretaña**	¿me da **se**-lyos pa-ra ... pos-**ta**-les pa-ra gran bre-**ta**-nya?
How much is it to send this parcel?	**¿Cuánto cuesta mandar este paquete?**	¿**kwan**to **kwes**ta man**dar es**te pa-**ke**-te?
How long will it take?	**¿Cuánto tarda en llegar?**	¿**kwan**to **tar**da en lye-**gar**?
by air/by priority post/by registered post	**por avión/por correo urgente/ por correo certificado**	por a-**byon**/por ko-**rre**-o oor-**khen**-te/por ko-**rre**-o thair-tee-fee-**ka**-do

YOU MAY HEAR...

Rellene este impreso re-**lye**-ne **es**te eem-**pre**-so	Fill in this form

> **Money** (p 91) > **Paying** (p 93)

Photos

You can usually get good prices in specialist photographic shops, particularly for camcorder equipment.

A video tape for this camcorder	**Una cinta para esta videocámara** **oo**na **theen**ta pa-ra **es**ta bee-de-o-**ka**-ma-ra
A memory card for this digital camera	**Una tarjeta de memoria para esta cámara digital** **oo**na tar-**khe**-ta de me-**mo**-ree-a pa-ra **es**ta **ka**-ma-ra dee-khee-**tal**
Have you batteries...?	**¿Tiene pilas...?** ¿**tye**-ne **pee**las...?
for this camera/ this camcorder	**para esta cámara/esta videocámara** pa-ra **es**ta **ka**-ma-ra/esta bee-de-o-**ka**-ma-ra
Is it OK to take pictures here?	**¿Se pueden hacer fotos aquí?** ¿se **pwe**-den a-**thair fo**-tos a-**kee**?
Would you take a picture of us, please?	**¿Podría hacernos una foto, por favor?** ¿po-**dree**-a a-**thair**-nos oona **fo**-to, por fa-**bor**?

Shopping

Leisure

Sightseeing and tourist office

The tourist office is called **la oficina de turismo**. If you are looking for somewhere to stay they should have details of hotels, campsites, etc. They also have free maps. Monday is not a good day for visiting museums, as this is the day they are generally closed.

Where is the tourist office?	**¿Dónde está la oficina de turismo?** ¿**don**de es**ta** la o-fee-**thee**-na de too-**rees**-mo?
What can we visit in the area?	**¿Qué podemos visitar en la zona?** ¿ke po-**de**-mos bee-see-**tar** en la **tho**-na?
Have you any leaflets?	**¿Tiene algún folleto?** ¿**tye**-ne al**goon** fo-**lye**-to?

Are there any excursions?	**¿Hay alguna excursión organizada?**	¿**a**ee al-**goo**-na eks-koor-**syon** or-ga-nee-**tha**-da?
We'd like to go to...	**Nos gustaría ir a...**	nos goos-ta-**ree**-a eer a...
How much does it cost to get in?	**¿Cuánto cuesta entrar?**	¿**kwan**to **kwes**ta en**trar**?
Are there any reductions for...?	**¿Hacen descuento a...?**	¿**a**-then des-**kwen**-to a...?
children	**los niños**	los **nee**-nyos
students	**los estudiantes**	los es-too-**dyan**-tes
unemployed	**los parados**	los pa-**ra**-dos
senior citizens	**los jubilados**	los khoo-bee-**la**-dos
over 60s	**mayores de sesenta**	ma-**yo**-res de se-**sen**-ta

> **Maps and guides** (p 65)

Entertainment

In large cities you can often find **La Guía del Ocio**, a magazine listing events and entertainment. Newspapers usually carry a page called **Agenda cultural** with local events.

What is there to do in the evenings?	**¿Qué se puede hacer por las noches?** ¿ke se **pwe**-de a-**thair** por las **no**-ches?
Is there anything for children?	**¿Hay algo para los niños?** ¿**a**ee **al**go **pa**-ra los **neen**yos?
I'd like ... tickets	**Quisiera ... entradas** kee-**sye**-ra ... en-**tra**-das
...adults	**...para mayores** ...pa-ra ma-**yo**-res
...children	**...para niños** ...pa-ra **neen**yos

YOU MAY HEAR...

La entrada cuesta ... euros con (derecho a) consumición la en-**tra**-da **kwes**ta ... **eoo**-ros kon (de-**re**-cho a) kon-soo-mee-**thyon**	It costs ... euros to get in including a free drink

Entertainment

Leisure/interests

Where can I/ we go...?	**¿Dónde se puede ir a...?** ¿**don**-de se **pwe**-de eer a...?
fishing	**pescar** pes**kar**
riding	**montar a caballo** mon**tar** a ka-**ba**-lyo
Are there any good beaches near here?	**¿Hay alguna playa buena cerca de aquí?** ¿**a**ee al-**goo**-na **pla**-ya **bwe**-na **thair**ka de a-**kee**?
Is there a swimming pool?	**¿Hay piscina?** ¿**a**ee pees-**thee**-na?

Music

There are often music and dance festivals in the summer. They generally begin quite late, at about 10.30 or 11 pm.

Are there any good concerts on?	**¿Dan algún buen concierto aquí?** ¿dan al**goon** bwen kon-**thyair**-to a-**kee**?

Where can I get tickets?	**¿Dónde venden las entradas?** ¿**don**de **ben**den las en-**tra**-das?
Where can we hear some flamenco/salsa?	**¿Qué sitios hay para escuchar flamenco/salsa?** ¿ke **see**tyos **a**ee pa-ra es-koo-**char** fla-**men**-ko/**sal**sa?

Cinema

The last film showing is usually at midnight and tickets are cheaper.

v.o (versión original) bair**syon** o-ree-khee-**nal**	original version

What's on at the cinema?	**¿Qué películas ponen?** ¿ke pe-**lee**-koo-las **po**-nen?
When does the film start?	**¿A qué hora empieza la película?** ¿a ke **o**-ra em-**pye**-tha la pe-**lee**-koo-la?
How much are the tickets?	**¿Cuánto cuestan las entradas?** ¿**kwan**to **kwes**tan las en-**tra**-das?

> **Making friends** (p 21)

Two for the (time) showing	**Dos para la sesión de las...** dos pa-ra la se-**syon** de las...

YOU MAY HEAR...	
Para la sala uno/dos no quedan localidades/entradas pa-ra la **sa**-la **oo**no/dos no **ke**-dan lo-ka-lee-**da**-des/ en-**tra**-das	For screen 1/2 there are no tickets left

Theatre/opera

Performances generally start late at about 9 or 10 pm.

el patio de butacas el **pa**-tyo de boo-**ta**-kas	stalls
la platea la pla-**te**-a	dress circle
el anfiteatro el an-fee-te-**a**-tro	upper circle
el palco el **pal**ko	box
la localidad/el asiento la lo-ka-lee-**dad/** el a-**syen**-to	seat

What's on at the theatre?	**¿Qué están echando en el teatro?**	¿ke es**tan** e-**chan**-do en el te-**a**-tro?
How do we get to the theatre?	**¿Cómo se va al teatro?**	¿**ko**-mo se ba al te-**a**-tro?
What prices are the tickets?	**¿De qué precios son las entradas?**	¿de ke pre-**thyos** son las en-**tra**-das?
I'd like two tickets...	**Quisiera dos entradas...**	kee-**sye**-ra dos en-**tra**-das...
for tonight	**para esta noche**	pa-ra **es**ta **no**-che
for tomorrow night	**para mañana por la noche**	pa-ra ma-**nya**-na por la **no**-che
for 5th August	**para el cinco de agosto**	pa-ra el **theen**ko de a-**go**-sto
in the stalls	**de patio de butacas**	de **pa**-tyo de boo-**ta**-kas
in the dress circle	**de platea**	de pla-**te**-a
in the upper circle	**de anfiteatro**	de an-fee-te-**a**-tro
When does the performance begin/end?	**¿Cúando empieza/termina la representación?**	¿**kwan**do em-**pye**-tha/tair-**mee**-na la re-pre-sen-ta-**thyon**?

Television

el mando (a distancia) el **man**do (a dees-**tan**-thya)	remote control
el telediario el te-le-dee-**a**-ryo	news
encender en-then-**dair**	to switch on
apagar a-pa-**gar**	to switch off
el programa el pro-**gra**-ma	programme
los dibujos animados los dee-**boo**-khos a-nee-**ma**-dos	cartoons

Where is the television?	**¿Dónde está el televisor?** ¿**don**de es**ta** el te-le-bee-**sor**?
How do you switch it on?	**¿Cómo se enciende?** ¿**ko**-mo se en-**thyen**-de?
Which button do I press?	**¿Qué botón tengo que pulsar?** ¿ke bo-**ton ten**go ke pool**sar**?
Please could you lower the volume?	**Por favor, ¿podría bajar el volumen?** por fa-**bor**, ¿po-**dree**-a ba-**khar** el bo-**loo**-men?
May I turn the volume up?	**¿Puedo subir el volumen?** ¿**pwe**-do soo**beer** el bo-**loo**-men?

When is the news?	**¿Cúando es el telediario?** ¿**kwan**do es el te-le-dee-**a**-ryo?
Do you have any English language channels?	**¿Hay alguna cadena en inglés?** ¿**a**ee al-**goo**-na ka-**de**-na en een**gles**?

Sport

The easiest way to buy tickets to a football match is direct from the stadium ticket booth about an hour before kick-off. Sunday matches usually begin between 5 and 6 pm. For big Saturday night matches you would have to buy tickets in advance. Saturday night matches usually begin about 9 pm.

Where can I/ we...?	**¿Dónde se puede...?** ¿**don**de se **pwe**-de...?
play tennis	**jugar al tenis** khoo**gar** al **te**-nees
play golf	**jugar al golf** khoo**gar** al golf
go swimming	**ir a nadar** eer a na-**dar**
go jogging	**hacer footing** a-**thair foo**teen

How much is it per hour?	**¿Cuánto cuesta la hora?** ¿**kwan**to **kwes**ta la **o**-ra?
Do you have to be a member?	**¿Hay que ser socio?** ¿**a**ee ke sair **so**-thyo?
Do they hire out...?	**¿Alquilan...?** ¿al-**kee**-lan...?
rackets	**raquetas** ra-**ke**-tas
golf clubs	**palos de golf** **pa**-los de golf
We'd like to go to see (name of team) play	**Nos gustaría ir a ver jugar al...** nos goos-ta-**ree**-a eer a bair khoo**gar** al...
Where can we get tickets?	**¿Dónde venden las entradas?** ¿**don**de **ben**den las en-**tra**-das?
How do we get to the stadium?	**¿Cómo se va al estadio?** ¿**ko**-mo se ba al es-**ta**-dyo?

Skiing

el forfait el for**fey**	ski pass
el monitor/la monitora el mo-nee-**tor**/ la mo-nee-**to**-ra	instructor
el esquí de fondo el es**kee** de **fon**do	cross-country skiing

I want to hire skis	**Querría alquilar unos esquíes**	ke-**rree**-a al-kee-**lar oo**nos es-**kee**-es
Does the price include...?	**¿El precio incluye...?**	¿el **pre**-thyo een-**kloo**-ye...?
boots	**las botas**	las **bo**-tas
poles	**los bastones**	los bas-**to**-nes
Can you adjust my bindings, please?	**¿Me puede ajustar las fijaciones?**	¿me **pwe**-de a-khoos-**tar** las fee-kha-**thyo**-nes?
How much is a pass...?	**¿Cuánto cuesta un forfait...?**	¿**kwan**to **kwes**ta oon for**fey**...?
for a day	**para un día**	pa-ra oon **dee**-a
per week	**semanal**	se-ma-**nal**
When does the last chair-lift go up?	**¿Cuándo sale el último telesilla?**	¿**kwan**do **sa**-le el **ool**-tee-mo te-le-**see**-lya?

YOU MAY HEAR...	
¿Ha esquiado alguna vez antes? ¿a es-kee-**a**-do al-**goo**-na beth **an**tes?	Have you ever skied before?
¿De qué largo quiere los esquíes? ¿de ke **lar**go **kye**-re los es-**kee**-es?	What length skis do you want?
¿Qué número de zapato usa? ¿ke **noo**-me-ro de tha-**pa**-to **oo**sa?	What is your shoe size?

Walking

Are there any guided walks?	**¿Organizan recorridos a pie con guía?**	¿or-ga-**nee**-than re-ko-**rree**-dos a pye kon **gee**-a?
Do you have a guide to local walks?	**¿Tiene alguna guía de esta zona que traiga recorridos a pie?**	¿**tye**-ne al-**goo**-na **gee**-a de **es**ta **tho**-na ke **traee**-ga re-ko-**rree**-dos a pye?
How many kilometres is the walk?	**¿De cuántos kilómetros es la excursión?**	¿de **kwan**tos kee-**lo**-me-tros es la eks-koor-**syon**?
How long will it take?	**¿Cuánto se tarda?**	¿**kwan**to se **tar**da?
Is it very steep?	**¿Hay mucha subida?**	¿**a**ee **moo**cha soo-**bee**-da?
We'd like to go climbing	**Nos gustaría hacer montañismo**	nos goos-ta-**ree**-a a-**thair** mon-ta-**nyees**-mo

> **Maps and guides** (p 65)

Communications

Telephone and mobile

To phone Spain from the UK, the international code is **00 34** plus the Spanish area code (e.g. Barcelona **93**, Madrid **91**) followed by the number you require. To phone the UK from Spain, dial **00 44** plus the UK area code without the first **0** e.g. Glasgow **(0)141**. For calls within Spain you must dial the area code and number (even for local calls).

A phonecard, please	**Una tarjeta telefónica, por favor** **oo**na tar-**khe**-ta te-le-**fo**-nee-ka, por fa-**bor**
for 6/12 euros	**de seis/doce euros** de seys/**do**-the **eoo**-ros
I want to make a phone call	**Quiero hacer una llamada telefónica** **kye**-ro a-**thair** **oo**na lya-**ma**-da te-le-**fo**-nee-ka
I will give you a call	**Te daré un toque** te da-**re** un **to**-ke

Where can I buy a phonecard?	**¿Dónde venden tarjetas telefónicas?**	¿**don**de **ben**den tar-**khe**-tas te-le-**fo**-nee-kas?
Do you have a mobile?	**¿Tiene móvil?**	¿**tye**-ne **mo**-beel?
What is the number of your mobile?	**¿Cuál es su número de móvil?**	¿kwal es soo **noo**-me-ro de **mo**-beel?
My mobile number is...	**Mi número de móvil es...**	mee **noo**-me-ro de **mo**-beel es...
Señor Lopez, please	**El Señor López, por favor**	el se-**nyor lo**-pez, por fa-**bor**
Extension (number)	**Extensión...**	eks-ten-**syon**...
Can I speak to...?	**¿Puedo hablar con...?**	¿**pwe**-do a-**blar** kon...?
I would like to speak to...	**Querría hablar con...**	ke-**rree**-a a-**blar** kon...
Can I speak to Mr Salas?	**¿Puedo hablar con el Sr. Salas?**	¿**pwe**-do a-**blar** kon el se-**nyor sa**-las?
Is Valle there?	**¿Está Valle?**	¿es**ta ba**-lye?

FACE TO FACE

A **¿Diga(me)?**
¿**di**-ga(-me)?
Hello

B **Querría hablar con ..., por favor**
ke-**rree**-a a-**blar** kon ..., por fa-**bor**
I'd like to speak to ..., please

A **¿De parte de quién?**
¿de **par**te de kyen?
Who's calling?

B **Soy Daniela**
soy da-**nye**-la
It's Daniela

A **Un momento, por favor**
oon mo-**men**-to, por fa-**bor**
Just a moment, please

This is Jim Brown	**Soy Jim Brown** soy jim brown
It's me	**Soy yo** soy yo
I want to make an outside call, can I have a line?	**Querría llamar fuera, ¿me da línea?** ke-**rree**-a lya-**mar fwe**-ra, ¿me da **lee**-ne-a?
I'll call back...	**Volveré a llamar...** bol-be-**re** a lya-**mar**...
later	**más tarde** mas **tar**de

tomorrow	**mañana** ma-**nya**-na

YOU MAY HEAR...	
¿Con quién hablo?/ ¿Quién es? ¿kon kyen **a**-blo/kyen es?	Who am I talking to?
No cuelgue, por favor no **kwel**ge, por fa-**bor**	Hold the line, please
Ahora se pone a-**o**-ra se **po**-ne	He/She is coming
Está comunicando es**ta** ko-moo-nee-**kan**-do	It's engaged
¿Puede volver a llamar más tarde? ¿**pwe**-de bol**bair** a lya-**mar** mas **tar**de?	Can you try again later?
Se ha equivocado de número se a e-kee-bo-**ka**-do de **noo**-me-ro	You have the wrong number
Deje su mensaje después de oír la señal (answering machine) **de**-khe soo men-**sa**-khe des**pwes** de o-**eer** la se-**nyal**	Please leave a message after the tone

YOU MAY HEAR...	
Por favor, se ruega apaguen los teléfonos móviles por fa-**bor**, se **rwe**-ga a-**pa**-gen los te-**le**-fo-nos **mo**-bee-les	Please turn your mobiles off

Text messaging

In mobile-phone messages accents and upside-down punctuation are often omitted.

I will text you	**Te mandaré un mensaje (al móvil)** te man-da-**re** oon men-**sa**-khe (al **mo**-beel)
Can you text me?	**¿Me puedes mandar un mensaje (al móvil)?** ¿me **pwe**-des man**dar** oon men-**sa**-khe (al **mo**-beel)?

tomorrow	**mñn (mañana)**
later	**+trd (más tarde)**
goodbye	**a2 (adiós)**
where?	**dnd? (¿dónde?)**

let's meet	**qdms? (¿quedamos?)**
how are you?	**q tl? (¿qué tal?)**
I'll see you soon	**TBL (te veo luego)**
I love you	**t q (te quiero)**
call me	**ymam (llámame)**
why?	**xq? (¿por qué?)**
are you coming?	**vns? (¿vienes?)**
because	**xq (porque)**

E-mail

New message:	**Nuevo mensaje:**
To:	**Para:**
From:	**De:**
Subject:	**Asunto:**
Forward:	**Reenviar:**
Inbox:	**Bandeja de entrada:**
Sent items:	**Enviados:**
Attachment:	**Archivo adjunto:**
Send:	**Enviar:**

Do you have an e-mail? **¿Tiene (dirección de) email?**
¿**tye**-ne (dee-rek-**thyon** de) ee-**meyl**?

E-mail

What is your e-mail address?	**¿Cuál es su (dirección de) email?** ¿kwal es soo (dee-rek-**thyon** de) ee-**meyl**?
How do you spell it?	**¿Cómo se escribe?** ¿**ko**-mo se es-**kree**-be?
All one word	**Todo junto** **to**-do **khoon**to
All lower case	**Todo en minúscula(s)** **to**-do en mee-**noos**-koo-la(s)
My e-mail address is...	**Mi (dirección de) email es...** mee (dee-rek-**thyon** de) ee-**meyl** es...
caroline.smith@bit.co.uk	**caroline punto smith arroba bit punto co punto uk** caroline **poon**to smith a-**rro**-ba bit **poon**to ko **poon**to oo ka
Can I send an e-mail?	**¿Puedo mandar un email?** ¿**pwe**-do man**dar** oon ee-**meyl**?
Did you get my e-mail?	**¿Le llegó mi email?** ¿le lye-**go** mee ee-**meyl**?

Internet

Are there any internet cafés here?	**¿Hay algún cibercafé aquí?** ¿**a**ee al**goon** thee-bair-ka-**fe** a-**kee**?
How much is it to log on for an hour?	**¿Cuánto cuesta una hora de conexión?** ¿**kwan**to **kwes**ta **oo**na **o**-ra de ko-nek-**syon**?
The website address is...	**La página (web) es...** la **pa**-khee-na (web) es...
www.collins.co.uk	**www.collins.co.uk** **oo**be **do**-ble **oo**be **do**-ble **oo**be **do**-ble **poon**to collins **poon**to ko **poon**to oo ka
I can't log on	**No puedo conectarme** no **pwe**-do ko-nek-**tar**-me

Fax

To fax Spain from the UK, the code is **00 34** followed by the Spanish area code, e.g. Madrid **91**, **Bilbao 94**, and the fax number.

Addressing a fax

de	from
a la atención de	for the attention of
fecha	date
con referencia a	re:
este documento contiene...	this document contains...
páginas, ésta inclusive	pages including this one

Do you have a fax?	**¿Tiene fax?** ¿**tye**-ne faks?
I want to send a fax	**Querría mandar un fax** ke-**rree**-a man**dar** oon faks
Please resend your fax	**Por favor, vuélvame a mandar su fax** por fa-**bor**, **bwel**-ba-me a man**dar** soo faks
I can't read it	**No se entiende** no se en-**tyen**-de

Communications

Practicalities

Money

Banks are generally open 8.30 am to 2 pm Monday to Friday, with some banks open on Saturday mornings. Double-check opening hours when you arrive as these change during the summer. The Spanish currency is the **euro** (**eoo**-ro). Euro cents are known as **céntimos** (**then**-tee-mos).

la tarjeta de crédito la tar-**khe**-ta de **kre**-dee-to	credit card
pagar en efectivo pa-**gar** en e-fek-**tee**-bo	pay in cash
la factura la fak-**too**-ra	invoice
los cheques de viaje los **che**-kes de **bya**-khe	traveller's cheques

Where can I/we change some money? — **¿Dónde se puede cambiar dinero?**
¿**don**de se **pwe**-de kam-**byar** dee-**ne**-ro?

I want to change these traveller's cheques	**Quiero cambiar estos cheques de viaje**	**kye**-ro kam**byar es**tos **che**-kes de **bya**-khe
When does the bank open/close?	**¿Cuándo abren/cierran el banco?**	¿**kwan**do **a**-bren/**thye**-rran el **ban**ko?
Can I pay with pounds/euros?	**¿Puedo pagar con libras/euros?**	¿**pwe**-do pa-**gar** kon **lee**bras/**eoo**-ros?
Where is the nearest cash dispenser?	**¿Dónde está el cajero más cercano?**	¿**don**de es**ta** el ka-**khe**-ro mas thair-**ka**-no?
Can I use my card with this cash dispenser?	**¿Puedo usar mi tarjeta en este cajero?**	¿**pwe**-do oo**sar** mee tar-**khe**-ta en **es**te ka-**khe**-ro?
Do you have any small change?	**¿Tiene suelto?**	¿**tye**-ne **swel**to?

Practicalities

Paying

el importe el eem-**por**-te	amount to be paid
la cuenta la **kwen**ta	bill
la factura la fak-**too**-ra	invoice
abone el importe en caja a-**bo**-ne el eem-**por**-te en **ka**-kha	pay at the cash desk
el tique (de compra) el **tee**ke de **kom**pra	till receipt

How much is it? **¿Cuánto es?**
¿**kwan**to es?

How much will it be? **¿Cuánto me costará?**
¿**kwan**to me kos-ta-**ra**?

Can I pay...? **¿Puedo pagar...?**
¿**pwe**-do pa-**gar**...?

by credit card **con tarjeta de crédito**
kon tar-**khe**-ta de **kre**-dee-to

by cheque **con talón/(un) cheque**
kon ta-**lon**/(oon) **che**-ke

Do you take credit cards? **¿Aceptan tarjetas de crédito?**
¿a-**thep**-tan tar-**khe**-tas de **kre**-dee-to?

Is VAT included? **¿Está incluido el IVA?**
¿Es**ta** een-kloo-**ee**-do el **ee**ba?

Put it on my bill **Póngalo en mi cuenta**
pon-ga-lo en mee **kwen**ta

I need a receipt, please	**Necesito un recibo, por favor** ne-the-**see**-to oon re-**thee**-bo, por fa-**bor**
Where do I pay?	**¿Dónde se paga?** ¿**Don**de se **pa**-ga?
I'm sorry	**Lo siento** lo **syen**to
I've nothing smaller	**No tengo cambio** no **ten**go **kam**byo

Luggage

consigna kon-**seeg**-na	left luggage office
consignas automáticas kon-**seeg**-nas ow-to-**ma**-tee-kas	luggage lockers
el carrito el ka-**rree**-to	luggage trolley

My luggage hasn't arrived	**Mi equipaje no ha llegado** mee e-kee-**pa**-khe no a lye-**ga**-do
My suitcase has arrived damaged	**La maleta ha llegado estropeada** la ma-**le**-ta a lye-**ga**-do es-tro-pe-**a**-da
What's happened to the luggage on the flight from...?	**¿Qué ha pasado con el equipaje del vuelo de...?** ¿ke a pa-**sa**-do kon el e-kee-**pa**-khe del **bwe**-lo de...?

> **Train** (p 32) > **Air travel** (p 38)

Repairs

Repairs while you wait are known as **reparaciones en el acto**.

This is broken	**Se me ha roto esto** se me a **ro**-to **es**to
Where can I get this repaired?	**¿Dónde me lo pueden arreglar?** ¿**don**de me lo **pwe**-den a-**rre**-glar?
Is it worth repairing?	**¿Merece la pena arreglarlo?** ¿me-**re**-the la **pe**-na a-rre-**glar**-lo?
Can you repair...?	**¿Puede arreglarme...?** ¿**pwe**-de a-rre-**glar**-me...?
these shoes	**estos zapatos** **es**tos tha-**pa**-tos
my watch	**el reloj** el re-**lokh**
How much will it be?	**¿Cuánto me costará?** ¿**kwan**to me kos-ta-**ra**?
Can you do it straightaway?	**¿Me lo puede hacer en el acto?** ¿me lo **pwe**-de a-**thair** en el **ak**to?
How long will it take to repair?	**¿Cuánto tardarán en arreglarlo?** ¿**kwan**to tar-da-**ran** en a-rre-**glar**-lo?

> **Breakdown** (p 45)

When will it be ready?	**¿Para cuándo estará?** ¿pa-ra **kwan**do es-ta-**ra**?

Laundry

la tintoreria la teen-to-re-**ree**-a	dry-cleaner's
la lavandería automática la la-ban-de-**ree**-a ow-to-**ma**-tee-ka	launderette
el detergente en polvo el de-tair-**khen**-te en **pol**vo	washing powder

Where can I do some washing?	**¿Dónde puedo lavar algo de ropa?** ¿**don**de **pwe**-do la-**bar al**go de **ro**-pa?
Is there a launderette near here?	**¿Hay alguna lavandería automática por aquí cerca?** ¿**a**ee al-**goo**-na la-ban-de-**ree**-a ow-to-**ma**-tee-ka por a-**kee thair**ka?
Is there somewhere to dry clothes?	**¿Hay algún sitio para secar la ropa?** ¿**a**ee al**goon see**tyo pa-ra se-**kar** la **ro**-pa?

Practicalities

Complaints

This doesn't work	**Esto no funciona**	**es**to no foon-**thyo**-na
The ... doesn't work	**El/La ... no funciona**	el/la ... no foon-**thyo**-na
The ... don't work	**Los/Las ... no funcionan**	los/las ... no foon-**thyo**-nan
light	**la luz**	la looth
heating	**la calefacción**	la ka-le-fak-**thyon**
air conditioning	**el aire acondicionado**	el **aee**-re a-kon-dee-thyo-**na**-do
There's a problem with the room	**Hay un problema con la habitación**	**a**ee oon pro-**ble**-ma kon la a-bee-ta-**thyon**
It's noisy	**Hay mucho ruido**	**a**ee **moo**cho **rwee**do
It's too hot (room)	**Hace demasiado calor**	**a**-the de-ma-**sya**-do ka-**lor**
It's too cold (room)	**Hace demasiado frío**	**a**-the de-ma-**sya**-do **free**-o
It's too hot/too cold (food)	**Está muy caliente/muy frío**	es**ta** mwee ka-**lyen**-te/mwee **free**-o

The meat is cold	**La carne está fría**	la **kar**ne es**ta free**-a
This isn't what I ordered	**Esto no es lo que yo he pedido**	**es**to no es lo ke yo e pe-**dee**-do
It's faulty	**Tiene un defecto**	**tye**-ne oon de-**fek**-to
It's dirty	**Está sucio**	es**ta soo**thyo
I want my money back	**Quiero que me devuelvan el dinero**	**kye**-ro ke me de-**bwel**-ban el dee-**ne**-ro

Problems

Can you help me?	**¿Me puede ayudar?**	¿me **pwe**-de a-yoo-**dar**?
I only speak a little Spanish	**Sólo hablo un poco de español**	**so**-lo **a**-blo oon **po**-ko de es-pa-**nyol**
Does anyone here speak English?	**¿Hay aquí alguien que hable inglés?**	¿**a**ee a-**kee al**gyen ke **a**-ble een**gles**?
What's the matter?	**¿Qué pasa?**	¿ke **pa**-sa?

Practicalities

I'm lost	**Me he perdido**	
	me e pair-**dee**-do	
How do I get to...?	**¿Cómo voy a...?**	
	¿**ko**-mo boy a...?	
I've missed...	**He perdido...**	
	e pair-**dee**-do...	
my train	**el tren**	
	el tren	
my plane	**el avión**	
	el a-**byon**	
my connection	**el enlace**	
	el en-**la**-the	
I've missed my flight because there was a strike	**He perdido el vuelo porque había una huelga**	
	e pair-**dee**-do el **bwe**-lo **por**ke a-**bee**-a **oo**na **wel**ga	
The coach has left without me	**Se ha ido el autocar y me ha dejado aquí**	
	se a **ee**do el ow-to-**kar** ee me a de-**kha**-do a-**kee**	
Can you show me how this works?	**¿Me puede enseñar como funciona esto?**	
	¿me **pwe**-de en-se-**nyar ko**-mo foon-**thyo**-na **es**to?	
I have lost my purse	**He perdido el monedero**	
	e pair-**dee**-do el mo-ne-**de**-ro	
I need to get to...	**Tengo que ir a...**	
	tengo ke eer a...	

Leave me alone!	**¡Déjeme en paz!** ¡**de**-khe-me en path!
Go away!	**¡Váyase!** ¡**ba**-ya-se!

Emergencies

The emergency number for the police is 091. If you need an ambulance, they will arrange it.

la policía la po-lee-**thee**-a	police
la ambulancia la am-boo-**lan**-thya	ambulance
los bomberos los bom-**be**-ros	fire brigade
urgencias oor-**khen**-thyas	casualty department

Help!	**¡Socorro!** ¡so-**ko**-rro!
Fire!	**¡Fuego!** ¡**fwe**-go!
There's been an accident	**Ha habido un accidente** a a-**bee**-do oon ak-thee-**den**-te
Someone is injured	**Hay un herido** **a**ee oon e-**ree**-do

Someone has been knocked down by a car	**Han atropellado a alguien**	an a-tro-pe-**lya**-do a **al**gyen
Call...	**Llame a...**	**lya**-me a...
the police	**la policía**	la po-lee-**thee**-a
an ambulance	**una ambulancia**	**oo**na am-boo-**lan**-thya
please	**por favor**	por fa-**bor**
Where is the police station?	**¿Dónde está la comisaría?**	¿**don**de es**ta** la ko-mee-sa-**ree**-a?
I want to report a theft	**Quiero denunciar un robo**	**kye**-ro de-noon-**thyar** oon **ro**-bo
I've been robbed/attacked	**Me han robado/agredido**	me an ro-**ba**-do/a-gre-**dee**-do
Someone's stolen my...	**Me han robado...**	me an ro-**ba**-do...
bag	**el bolso**	el **bol**so
traveller's cheques	**los cheques de viaje**	los **che**-kes de **bya**-khe
My car has been broken into	**Me han entrado en el coche**	me an en-**tra**-do en el **ko**-che
My car has been stolen	**Me han robado el coche**	me an ro-**ba**-do el **ko**-che
I've been raped	**Me han violado**	me an byo-**la**-do

I want to speak to a policewoman	**Quiero hablar con una mujer policía** **kye**-ro a-**blar** kon **oo**na moo**khair** po-lee-**thee**-a
I need to make an urgent telephone call	**Necesito hacer una llamada urgente** ne-the-**see**-to a-**thair oo**na lya-**ma**-da oor-**khen**-te
I need a report for my insurance	**Necesito un informe para el seguro** ne-the-**see**-to oon een-**for**-me pa-ra el se-**goo**-ro
How much is the fine?	**¿De cuánto es la multa?** ¿de **kwan**to es la **mool**ta?
Where do I pay it?	**¿Dónde la pago?** ¿**don**de la **pa**-go?
Do I have to pay it straightaway?	**¿Tengo que pagarla inmediatamente?** ¿**ten**go ke pa-**gar**-la een-me-dya-ta-**men**-te?
I'm very sorry	**Lo siento mucho** lo **syen**to **moo**cho

Practicalities

YOU MAY HEAR...	
Se ha saltado el semáforo en rojo se a sal-**ta**-do el se-**ma**-fo-ro en **ro**-kho	You went through a red light

Health

Pharmacy

la farmacia la far-**ma**-thya	pharmacy/chemist
la farmacia de guardia la far-**ma**-thya de **gwar**dya	duty chemist
la receta médica la re-**the**-ta **me**-dee-ka	prescription

Have you something for...?	**¿Tiene algo para...?** ¿**tye**-ne **al**go pa-ra...?
a headache	**el dolor de cabeza** el do-**lor** de ka-**be**-tha
car sickness	**el mareo** el ma-**re**-o
diarrhoea	**la diarrea** la dee-a-**rre**-a
I have a rash	**Me ha salido un sarpullido** me a sa-**lee**-do oon sar-poo-**lyee**-do
I feel sick	**Tengo naúseas** **ten**go **now**-se-as

Is it safe for children?	**¿Lo pueden tomar los niños?** ¿lo **pwe**-den to-**mar** los **nee**nyos?
How much should I give?	**¿Cuánto le doy?** ¿**kwan**to le doy?

YOU MAY HEAR...

Tómelo tres veces al día antes de/con/después de las comidas **to**-me-lo tres **be**-thes al **dee**-a **an**tes de/kon/ des**pwes** de las ko-**mee**-das	Take it three times a day before/with/ after meals

Body

In Spanish the possessive (my, his, her, etc.) is generally not used with parts of the body, e.g.

My head hurts	**Me duele la cabeza**
My hands are dirty	**Tengo las manos sucias**

ankle	**el tobillo**	to-**bee**-lyo
arm	**el brazo**	**bra**-tho
back	**la espalda**	es-**pal**-da

Health

bone	**el hueso**	**we**-so
ear	**la oreja/el oído**	o-**re**-kha/o-**ee**-do
eye	**el ojo**	**o**-kho
finger	**el dedo**	**de**-do
foot	**el pie**	pye
hand	**la mano**	**ma**-no
head	**la cabeza**	ka-**be**-tha
heart	**el corazón**	ko-ra-**thon**
hip	**la cadera**	ka-**de**-ra
kidney	**el riñón**	ree**nyon**
knee	**la rodilla**	ro-**dee**-lya
leg	**la pierna**	**pyair**na
liver	**el hígado**	**ee**-ga-do
mouth	**la boca**	**bo**-ka
nail	**la uña**	**oo**nya
neck	**el cuello**	**kwe**-lyo
nose	**la nariz**	na-**reeth**
stomach	**el estómago**	es-**to**-ma-go
throat	**la garganta**	gar-**gan**-ta
toe	**el dedo del pie**	**de**-do del pye
wrist	**la muñeca**	moo-**nye**-ka

Doctor

If you need to see a doctor, simply visit the nearest clinic with your E111 card and ask for an appointment. You usually need to go in the morning (9 am) to get a ticket for an appointment later in the day.

FACE TO FACE

A **¿Qué le pasa/ocurre?**
¿ke le **pa**-sa/o-**koo**-rre?
What's wrong?

B **Me encuentro mal/No me encuentro bien**
me en-**kwen**-tro mal/no me en-**kwen**-tro byen
I feel ill

A **¿Tiene fiebre?**
¿**tye**-ne **fye**-bre?
Do you have a temperature?

B **No, me duele aquí**
no, me **dwe**-le a-**kee**
No, I have a pain here *(point)*

I need a doctor	**Necesito un médico** ne-the-**see**-to oon **me**-dee-ko
My son/daughter is ill	**Mi hijo/hija está enfermo(a)** mee **ee**kho/**ee**kha es**ta** en-**fair**-mo(a)
He/She has a temperature	**Tiene fiebre** **tye**-ne **fye**-bre

Health

I'm diabetic	**Soy diabético(a)** soy dya-**be**-tee-ko(a)
I'm pregnant	**Estoy embarazada** es**toy** em-ba-ra-**tha**-da
I'm on the pill	**Tomo la píldora** **to**-mo la **peel**-do-ra
I'm allergic to penicillin	**Soy alérgico(a) a la penicilina** soy a-**lair**-khee-ko(a) a la pe-nee-thee-**lee**-na
My blood group is...	**Mi grupo sanguíneo es...** mee **groo**po san-**gee**-ne-o es...
Will he/she have to go to hospital?	**¿Tendrá que ir al hospital?** ¿ten**dra** ke eer al os-pee-**tal**?
Will I have to pay?	**¿Tengo que pagar?** ¿**ten**go ke pa-**gar**?
How much will it cost?	**¿Cuánto va a costar?** ¿**kwan**to ba a kost**ar**?
I need a receipt for the insurance	**Necesito un recibo para el seguro** ne-the-**see**-to oon re-**thee**-bo pa-ra el se-**goo**-ro

YOU MAY HEAR...

Tiene que ingresar **tye**-ne ke een-gre-**sar**	You will have to be admitted to hospital
No es grave no es **gra**-ve	It's not serious

Doctor

> **Emergencies** (p 100)

Dentist

All dental provision is private. Simply book an appointment. It is advisable to get a quote in advance for any work to be done.

el empaste el em-**pas**-te	filling
la funda la **foon**da	crown
la dentadura postiza la den-ta-**doo**-ra pos-**tee**-tha	dentures

I need a dentist	**Necesito un dentista** ne-the-**see**-to oon den-**tees**-ta
He/She has toothache	**Tiene dolor de muelas** **tye**-ne do-**lor** de **mwe**-las
Can you do a temporary filling?	**¿Puede hacer un empaste provisional?** ¿**pwe**-de a-**thair** oon em-**pas**-te pro-bee-syo-**nal**?
It hurts (me)	**Me duele** me **dwe**-le
Can you give me something for the pain?	**¿Puede darme algo para el dolor?** ¿**pwe**-de **dar**me **al**go pa-ra el do-**lor**?

Health

Can you repair my dentures?	**¿Puede arreglarme la dentadura postiza?**	¿**pwe**-de a-rre-**glar**-me la den-ta-**doo**-ra pos-**tee**-tha?
Do I have to pay?	**¿Tengo que pagar?**	¿**ten**go ke pa-**gar**?
How much will it be?	**¿Cuánto me va a costar?**	¿**kwan**to me ba a kos**tar**?

YOU MAY HEAR...	
Hay que sacarla **a**ee ke sa-**kar**-la	It has to come out
Voy a ponerle una inyección boy a po-**nair**-le **oo**na een-yek-**thyon**	I'm going to give you an injection

Different types of travellers

Disabled travellers

What facilities do you have for disabled people?	**¿Qué instalaciones tienen para minusválidos?** ¿ke eens-ta-la-**thyo**-nes **tye**-nen pa-ra mee-noos-**ba**-lee-dos?
Are there any toilets for the disabled?	**¿Hay aseos para minusválidos?** ¿**a**ee a-**se**-os pa-ra mee-noos-**ba**-lee-dos?
Do you have any bedrooms on the ground floor?	**¿Tienen alguna habitación en la planta baja?** ¿**tye**-nen al-**goo**-na a-bee-ta-**thyon** en la **plan**ta **ba**-kha?
Is there a lift?	**¿Hay ascensor?** ¿**a**ee as-then-**sor**?
Where is the lift?	**¿Dónde está el ascensor?** ¿**don**de es**ta** el as-then-**sor**?
Is there an induction loop?	**¿Hay audífonos?** ¿**a**ee ow-**dee**-fo-nos?
Do you have wheelchairs?	**¿Tienen sillas de ruedas?** ¿**tye**-nen **see**lyas de **rwe**-das?

> **Hotel (booking)** (p 50)

Can you visit ... in a wheelchair?	**¿Se puede visitar ... en silla de ruedas?** ¿se **pwe**-de bee-see-**tar** ... en **see**lya de **rwe**-das?
Is there a reduction for disabled people?	**¿Hacen descuento a los minusválidos?** ¿**a**-then des-**kwen**-to a los mee-noos-**ba**-lee-dos?
Is there somewhere I can sit down?	**¿Hay algún sitio donde pueda sentarme?** ¿**a**ee al**goon see**tyo **don**de **pwe**-da sen-**tar**-me?

With kids

Public transport is free for children under 4. Children between 4 and 12 pay half price.

A child's ticket	**Un billete de niño** oon bee-**lye**-te de **neen**yo
He/She is ... years old	**Tiene ... años** **tye**-ne ... **a**-nyos
Is there a reduction for children?	**¿Hay descuento para niños?** ¿**a**ee des-**kwen**-to pa-ra **nee**nyos?
Do you have a children's menu?	**¿Tiene menú para niños?** ¿**tye**-ne me-**noo** pa-ra **nee**nyos?

Is it OK to take children?	**¿Está permitido llevar niños?** ¿es**ta** pair-mee-**tee**-do **lye**-bar **nee**nyos?
What is there for children to do?	**¿Qué cosas hay para los niños?** ¿ke **ko**-sas **a**ee pa-ra los **nee**nyos?
Is there a play park near here?	**¿Hay algún parque infantil por aquí cerca?** ¿**a**ee al**goon par**ke een-fan-**teel** por a-**kee thair**ka?
Is it safe for children?	**¿Es seguro para los niños?** ¿es se-**goo**-ro pa-ra los **nee**nyos?
Do you have...?	**¿Tiene...?** ¿**tye**-ne...?
a high chair	**una trona** **oo**na **tro**-na
a cot	**una cuna** **oo**na **koo**na
I have two children	**Tengo dos hijos** **ten**go dos **ee**khos
He/She is 10 years old	**Tiene diez años** **tye**-ne dyeth **a**-nyos

> **Doctor** (p 106)

Reference

Alphabet

The Spanish alphabet treats **ch**, **ll** and **ñ** as separate letters. Below are the words used for clarification when spelling something out.

¿Cómo se escribe? ¿**ko**-mo se es-**kree**-be?	How do you spell it?
A de Antonio, B de Barcelona a de an-**to**-nyo, be de bar-the-**lo**-na	A for Antonio, B for Barcelona

A	a	**Antonio**	an-**to**-nyo
B	be	**Barcelona**	bar-the-**lo**-na
C	the	**Carmen**	**kar**men
CH	che	**Chocolate**	cho-ko-**la**-te
D	de	**Dolores**	do-**lo**-res
E	e	**Enrique**	en-**rree**-ke
F	**e**-fe	**Francia**	**fran**thya
G	khe	**Gerona**	khe-**ro**-na

H	**a**-che	**Historia**	ees-**to**-rya
I	ee	**Inés**	ee**nes**
J	**kho**-ta	**José**	kho-**se**
K	ka	**Kilo**	**kee**lo
L	**e**-le	**Lorenzo**	lo-**ren**-tho
LL	**e**-lye	**Lluvia**	**lyoo**bya
M	**e**-me	**Madrid**	ma-**dreed**
N	**e**-ne	**Navarra**	na-**ba**-rra
Ñ	**e**-nye	**Ñoño**	**nyo**-nyo
O	o	**Oviedo**	o-**bye**-do
P	pe	**París**	pa-**rees**
Q	koo	**Querido**	ke-**ree**-do
R	**e**-re	**Carta**	**kar**ta
RR	**e**-rre	**Carrete**	ka-**rre**-te
S	**e**-se	**Sábado**	**sa**-ba-do
T	te	**Tarragona**	ta-rra-**go**-na
U	oo	**Ulises**	oo-**lee**-ses
V	**oo**be	**Valencia**	ba-**len**-thya
W	**oo**be **do**-ble	**Washington**	**wa**-seen-ton
X	**e**-kees	**Xilófono**	see-**lo**-fo-no
Y	ee **grye**-ga	**Yegua**	**ye**-gwa
Z	**the**-ta	**Zaragoza**	tha-ra-**go**-tha

Measurements and quantities

1 lb = approx. 0.5 kilo – 1 pint = approx. 0.5 litre

Liquids

1/2 litre of...	**medio litro de...** **me**-dyo **lee**tro de...
a litre of...	**un litro de...** oon **lee**tro de...
1/2 bottle of...	**media botella de...** **me**-dya bo-**te**-lya de...
a bottle of...	**una botella de...** **oo**na bo-**te**-lya de...
a glass of...	**un vaso de...** oon **ba**-so de...

Weights

100 grams of...	**cien gramos de...** thyen **gra**-mos de...
1/2 kilo of...	**medio kilo de...** **me**-dyo **kee**lo de...
a kilo of...	**un kilo de...** oon **kee**lo de...

Food

a slice of...	**una loncha de...**	**oo**na **lon**cha de...
a portion of...	**una ración de...**	**oo**na ra-**thyon** de...
a dozen...	**una docena de...**	**oo**na do-**the**-na de...
a box of...	**una caja de...**	**oo**na **ka**-kha de...
a packet of...	**un paquete de...**	oon pa-**ke**-te de...
a tin of...	**una lata de...**	**oo**na **la**-ta de...
a jar of...	**un tarro de...**	oon **ta**-rro de...

Miscellaneous

10 euros worth of...	**diez euros de...**	dyeth **eoo**-ros de...
a quarter	**un cuarto**	oon **kwar**to
ten per cent	**el diez por ciento**	el dyeth por **thyen**to
more...	**más...**	mas...
less...	**menos...**	**me**-nos...
enough	**bastante**	bas-**tan**-te
double	**el doble**	el **do**-ble
twice	**dos veces**	dos **be**-thes

Numbers

0 **cero** **the**-ro
1 **uno** **oo**no
2 **dos** dos
3 **tres** tres
4 **cuatro** **kwa**-tro
5 **cinco** **theen**ko
6 **seis** seys
7 **siete** **sye**-te
8 **ocho** **o**-cho
9 **nueve** **nwe**-be
10 **diez** dyeth
11 **once** **on**the
12 **doce** **do**-the
13 **trece** **tre**-the
14 **catorce** ka-**tor**-the
15 **quince** **keen**the
16 **dieciséis** dye-thee-**seys**
17 **diecisiete** dye-thee-**sye**-te
18 **dieciocho** dye-thee-**o**-cho
19 **diecinueve** dye-thee-**nwe**-be
20 **veinte** **beyn**te
21 **veintiuno** beyn-tee-**oo**-no
22 **veintidós** beyn-tee-**dos**
23 **veintitrés** beyn-tee-**tres**
24 **veinticuatro** beyn-tee-**kwa**-tro

30	**treinta** **treyn**ta
40	**cuarenta** kwa-**ren**-ta
50	**cincuenta** theen-**kwen**-ta
60	**sesenta** se-**sen**-ta
70	**setenta** se-**ten**-ta
80	**ochenta** o-**chen**-ta
90	**noventa** no-**ben**-ta
100	**cien** thyen
110	**ciento diez** **thyen**to dyeth
500	**quinientos** kee-**nyen**-tos
1,000	**mil** meel
2,000	**dos mil** dos meel
1 million	**un millón** oon mee**lyon**

1st	**primer(o) 1er/1º** pree-**me**-ro	6th	**sexto 6º** **seks**to
2nd	**segundo 2º** se-**goon**-do	7th	**séptimo 7º** **sep**-tee-mo
3rd	**tercer(o) 3er/3º** tair-**the**-ro	8th	**octavo 8º** ok-**ta**-bo
4th	**cuarto 4º** **kwar**to	9th	**noveno 9º** no-**be**-no
5th	**quinto 5º** **keen**to	10th	**décimo 10º** **de**-thee-mo

Days and months

Days

Monday	**lunes**	**loo**nes
Tuesday	**martes**	**mar**tes
Wednesday	**miércoles**	**myair**-ko-les
Thursday	**jueves**	**khwe**-bes
Friday	**viernes**	**byair**nes
Saturday	**sábado**	**sa**-ba-do
Sunday	**domingo**	do-**meen**-go

Months

January	**enero**	e-**ne**-ro
February	**febrero**	fe-**bre**-ro
March	**marzo**	**mar**tho
April	**abril**	a-**breel**
May	**mayo**	**ma**-yo
June	**junio**	**khoo**nyo
July	**julio**	**khoo**lyo
August	**agosto**	a-**gos**-to
September	**septiembre**	sep-**tyem**-bre
October	**octubre**	ok-**too**-bre
November	**noviembre**	no-**byem**-bre
December	**diciembre**	dee-**thyem**-bre

Seasons

spring	**la primavera**	la pree-ma-**be**-ra
summer	**el verano**	el be-**ra**-no
autumn	**el otoño**	el o-**to**-nyo
winter	**el invierno**	el een-**byair**-no

What is today's date?	**¿Qué fecha es hoy?** ¿ke **fe**-cha es oy?
What day is it today?	**¿Qué día es hoy?** ¿ke **dee**-a es oy?
It's the 5th of July 2006	**Es cinco de julio de dos mil seis** es **theen**ko de **khoo**lyo de dos meel seys
on Saturday	**el sábado** el **sa**-ba-do
on Saturdays	**los sábados** los **sa**-ba-dos
every Saturday	**todos los sábados** **to**-dos los **sa**-ba-dos
this Saturday	**este sábado** **es**te **sa**-ba-do
next Saturday	**el sábado que viene** el **sa**-ba-do ke **bye**-ne
last Saturday	**el sábado pasado** el **sa**-ba-do pa-**sa**-do
in June	**en junio** en **khoo**nyo

at the beginning of June	**a primeros de junio**	a pree-**me**-ros de **khoo**nyo
at the end of June	**a finales de junio**	a fee-**na**-les de **khoo**nyo
before summer	**antes del verano**	**an**tes del be-**ra**-no
during the summer	**en el verano**	en el be-**ra**-no
after summer	**después del verano**	des**pwes** del be-**ra**-no

Time

The 24-hour clock is used a lot more in Europe than in Britain. After 1200 midday, it continues: **1300 – las trece**, **1400 – las catorce**, **1500 – las quince**, etc. until **2400 – las veinticuatro**. With the 24-hour clock, the words **cuarto** (quarter) and **media** (half) aren't used:

13:15 (1.15 pm)	**las trece quince/ (la una y cuarto)**
19:30 (7.30 pm)	**las diecinueve treinta/ (las siete y media)**
22:45 (10.45 pm)	**las veintidós cuarenta y cinco/ (las once menos cuarto)**

What time is it, please?	**¿Qué hora es, por favor?** ¿ke **o**-ra es, por fa-**bor**?
am	**de la mañana** de la ma-**nya**-na
pm	**de la tarde** de la **tar**de
It's...	**Son...** son...
2 o'clock	**las dos** las dos
3 o'clock	**las tres** las tres
6 o'clock (etc.)	**las seis** las seys
It's 1 o'clock	**Es la una** es la **oo**na
It's 1200 midday	**Son las doce del mediodía** son las **do**-the del me-dyo-**dee**-a
At midnight	**A medianoche** a me-dya-**no**-che
9	**las nueve** las **nwe**-be
9.10	**las nueve y diez** las **nwe**-be ee dyeth
quarter past 9	**las nueve y cuarto** las **nwe**-be ee **kwar**to
9.20	**las nueve y veinte** las **nwe**-be ee **beyn**te

Reference

9.30	**las nueve y media** las **nwe**-be ee **me**-dya
9.35	**las diez menos veinticinco** las dyeth **me**-nos beyn-tee-**theen**-ko
quarter to 10	**las diez menos cuarto** las dyeth **me**-nos **kwar**to
10 to 10	**las diez menos diez** las dyeth **me**-nos dyeth

Time phrases

When does it open/close?	**¿Cuándo abre/cierra?** ¿**kwan**do **a**-bre/**thye**-rra?
When does it begin/finish?	**¿Cuándo empieza/termina?** ¿**kwan**do em-**pye**-tha/ tair-**mee**-na?
at 3 o'clock	**a las tres** a las tres
before 3 o'clock	**antes de las tres** **an**tes de las tres
after 3 o'clock	**después de las tres** des**pwes** de las tres
today	**hoy** oy

tonight	**esta noche** **es**ta **no**-che
tomorrow	**mañana** ma-**nya**-na
yesterday	**ayer** a-**yair**
in the morning	**por la mañana** por la ma-**nya**-na
this morning	**esta mañana** **es**ta ma-**nya**-na
in the afternoon	**por la tarde** (until dusk) por la **tar**de
in the evening	**por la tarde/por la noche** (late evening or night) por la **tar**de/por la **no**-che

Eating out

Eating places

Tapas A popular and inexpensive venue is the Tapas bar – you'll find these wherever you go. It is a good way of trying out different foods.

Cafetería Normally serves some hot dishes as well as toasted sandwiches (**sándwiches**) and cakes (**pasteles**).

Panadería Bakery. They often sell snacks and sweets.

Pastelería Cake shop

Confitería Cake shop

Bodega A wine cellar. Rather like a wine bar which serves food.

Restaurante Mealtimes are late in Spain. Lunch is generally served from 1 to 4.30 pm and dinner from 8 to 11.30 pm. The menu is usually displayed outside.

Chiringuito Beach bar/café

Mesón Traditional-style tavern restaurant.

Heladería Ice-cream parlour which also serves milkshakes: **batidos**.

In a bar/café

If you want a strong black coffee ask for **un café solo**. For a white coffee ask for **un café con leche**. Tea in Spain tends to be served weak and with lemon. And be careful not to ask for tea with milk, as it is likely that the tea bag would be put straight into hot milk. It is best to ask for the milk served separately (**aparte**).

FACE TO FACE

¿Qué desea?/¿Qué va a tomar?
¿ke de-**se**-a?/¿ke ba a to-**mar**?
What will you have?

Un café con leche, por favor
oon ka-**fe** kon **le**-che, por fa-**bor**
A white coffee, please

a coffee	**un café** oon ka-**fe**
a lager	**una cerveza** **oo**na thair-**be**-tha
a dry sherry	**un fino** oon **fee**no
...please	**...por favor** ...por fa-**bor**
a tea...	**un té...** oon te...
with the milk apart	**con la leche aparte** kon la **le**-che a-**par**-te
with lemon	**con limón** kon lee**mon**
for two	**para dos** pa-ra dos
for me	**para mí** pa-ra mee

for him/her	**para él/ella** pa-ra el/**e**-lya
for us	**para nosotros** pa-ra no-**so**-tros
with ice, please	**con hielo, por favor** kon **ye**-lo, por fa-**bor**
no sugar	**sin azúcar** seen a-**thoo**-kar
Have you sweetener?	**¿Tiene sacarina?** ¿**tye**-ne sa-ka-**ree**-na?
A bottle of mineral water	**Una botella de agua mineral** **oo**na bo-**te**-lya de **a**-gwa mee-ne-**ral**
sparkling	**con gas** kon gas
still	**sin gas** sin gas

Other drinks to try

un café con hielo iced coffee
un chocolate rich-tasting hot chocolate, often served with **churros**
una horchata refreshing tiger nut (chufa nut) milk
un zumo juice: **de melocotón** peach, **de tomate** tomato
un anís aniseed apéritif
un batido milkshake: **de chocolate** chocolate, **de fresa** strawberry, **de vainilla** vanilla

Reading the menu

Restaurants will usually have the menu displayed next to the entrance. If you don't want a full meal, **tapas** are an ideal way of trying out the different tastes of Spain. A list of **tapas** can be found on page 137.

platos combinados usually meat or fish served with rice, chips or potatoes and vegetables

menú del día 3-course meal often including wine

desayunos y meriendas breakfasts and snacks

tapas y raciones tapas and portions. Portions are a larger helping of tapas

la carta	menu
entremeses	starters
sopas	soups
ensalada	salads
carnes	meat
pescados	fish
huevos	egg dishes
revueltos	scrambled egg cooked with mushroom, spinach or asparagus

pastas	pasta
arroz	rice dishes
quesos	cheese
postres	desserts
bebidas	drinks

In a restaurant

If you are vegetarian, or prefer vegetarian dishes, turn to the VEGETARIAN topic on page 132 for further phrases.

The menu, please	**La carta, por favor** la **kar**ta, por fa-**bor**
What is the dish of the day?	**¿Cuál es el plato del día?** ¿kwal es el **pla**-to del **dee**-a?
Do you have...?	**¿Tienen...?** ¿**tye**-nen...?
a set-price menu	**menú del día** me-**noo** del **dee**-a
a children's menu	**menú para niños** me-**noo** pa-ra **nee**nyos
Can you recommend a local dish?	**¿Puede recomendar algún plato típico de aquí?** ¿**pwe**-de re-ko-men-**dar** al**goon** **pla**-to **tee**-pee-ko de a-**kee**?

Eating out

FACE TO FACE

Querría reservar una mesa para ... personas
ke-**rree**-a re-sair-**bar oo**-na **me**-sa pa-ra ... pair-**so**-nas
I'd like to book a table for ... people

¿Para cuándo?
¿pa-ra **kwan**do?
When for?

Para esta noche .../para mañana por la noche .../a las ocho
pa-ra **es**ta **no**-che .../pa-ra ma-**nya**-na por la **no**-che .../a las **o**-cho
for tonight .../for tomorrow night .../at 8 o'clock

What is in this?	**¿Qué lleva este plato?** ¿ke **lye**-ba **es**te **pla**-to?
I'll have this (point at menu)	**Voy a tomar esto** boy a to-**mar es**to
Excuse me!	**¡Oiga, por favor!** ¡**oy**ga, por fa-**bor**!
Please bring...	**¿Nos trae...?** ¿nos **tra**-e...?
more bread	**más pan** mas pan
more water	**más agua** mas **a**-gwa
another bottle	**otra botella** **o**-tra bo-**te**-lya

the bill	**la cuenta** la **kwen**ta
Is service included?	**¿Está incluido el servicio?** ¿es**ta** een-kloo-**ee**-do el sair-**bee**-thyo?

Vegetarian

Don't expect great things – the Spanish love good meat!

Are there any vegetarian restaurants here?	**¿Hay algún restaurante vegetariano aquí?** ¿**a**ee al**goon** res-tow-**ran**-te be-khe-ta-**rya**-no a-**kee**?
Do you have any vegetarian dishes?	**¿Tienen algún plato vegetariano?** ¿**tye**-nen al**goon** **pla**-to be-khe-ta-**rya**-no?
Which dishes have no meat/fish?	**¿Cuáles son los platos que no llevan carne/pescado?** ¿**kwa**-les son los **pla**-tos que no **lye**-ban **kar**ne/pes-**ka**-do?
What fish dishes do you have?	**¿Qué tienen de pescado?** ¿ke **tye**-nen de pes-**ka**-do?

I'd like pasta as a starter	**De primero, quisiera tomar pasta**	de pree-**me**-ro, kee-**sye**-ra to-**mar pas**ta
I don't like meat	**No me gusta la carne**	no me **goos**ta la **kar**ne
What do you recommend?	**¿Qué me recomienda?**	¿ke me re-ko-**myen**-da?
Is it made with vegetable stock?	**¿Está hecho con caldo de verduras?**	¿es**ta e**-cho kon **kal**do de bair-**doo**-ras?

Possible dishes

berenjenas aubergines
ensalada salad
espárragos asparagus
gazpacho cold cucumber, peppers, garlic and tomato soup
pisto peppers, courgettes, onions cooked in a tomato sauce
judías verdes French beans
revuelto de champiñones mushrooms with scrambled eggs
revuelto de espinacas spinach with scrambled eggs
tortilla española omelette with potato and onions

Wines and spirits

The wine list, please	**La carta de vinos, por favor** la **kar**ta de **bee**nos, por fa-**bor**
Can you recommend a good wine?	**¿Puede recomendar un buen vino?** ¿**pwe**-de re-ko-men-**dar** oon bwen **bee**no?
A bottle...	**Una botella...** **oo**na bo-**te**-lya...
A carafe...	**Una jarra...** **oo**na **kha**-rra...
of the house wine	**de vino de la casa** de **bee**no de la **ka**-sa
of red wine	**de vino tinto** de **bee**no **teen**to
of white wine	**de vino blanco** de **bee**no **blan**ko

Wines

Albariño smooth white wine from Galicia
Alella dry, medium-dry white wines from Cataluña
Alicante strong country reds and **Fondillón**, aged mature wine
Cariñena mainly red wines, best drunk young, from Aragón

Cava good quality sparkling white wine from Penedés (similar to Champagne)
Cigales light, fruity, dry rosé wines from Castilla-León
Jumilla strong, dark red wines from Murcia
Lágrima one of the best of the **Málaga** wines, very sweet
La Mancha firm whites and reds from Castilla-La Mancha
Málaga fortified, sweet, dark dessert wine
Navarra full-bodied reds from Navarra
Penedés fine reds, rosés and whites. Home of **Cava**
Ribeiro young, fresh, white wines from Galicia
Ribera del Duero fruity rosés and deep distinguished reds from the banks of the river Duero in Castilla-León
Rioja some of the finest red wines of Spain: full-bodied, rich and aged in oak. Also good white Riojas aged in oak
Valdepeñas soft, fruity, red wines and white wines

Types of sherry

Jerez sherry
Fino light, dry sherry, usually served chilled as an apéritif
Amontillado dry, nutty, amber sherry made from matured **fino**

Oloroso a dark, rich sherry which has been aged. It is often sweetened and sold as a cream sherry
Palo cortado midway between an **oloroso** and a **fino**

Other drinks

What liqueurs do you have?	**¿Qué licores tienen?** ¿ke lee-**ko**-res **tye**-nen?

Anís aniseed-flavoured liqueur
Coñac Spanish brandy
Orujo strong spirit made from grape pressings
Pacharán sloe brandy
Ron rum
Sidra dry cider from Asturias

Menu reader

Drinks and tapas

There are many different varieties of **tapas** depending on the region. A larger portion of **tapas** is called a **ración**. A **pincho** is a **tapa** on a cocktail stick.

aceite oil
  aceite de oliva olive oil
aceitunas olives
  aceitunas rellenas stuffed olives
adobo, ...en marinated
agua water
  agua mineral mineral water
  agua con gas sparkling water
  agua sin gas still water
ahumado smoked
ajillo, ...al with garlic
ajo garlic
albaricoque apricot
albóndigas meatballs in sauce
alcachofas artichokes
aliño dressing

alioli/allioli olive oil and garlic mashed together into a creamy paste similar to mayonnaise. Served with meat, potatoes or fish

almejas clams

almejas a la marinera steamed clams cooked with parsley, wine and garlic

almendras almonds

alubias large white beans found in many stews

anchoa anchovy

anguila eel

angulas baby eels, highly prized

arenque herring

arroz rice

arroz a la cubana rice with fried egg and tomato sauce

arroz con leche rice pudding flavoured with cinnamon

arroz negro black rice (with squid in its own ink)

asado roasted

asadillo roasted sliced red peppers in olive oil and garlic

atún tuna (usually fresh)

avellana hazelnut

bacalao salt cod, cod

bacalao a la vizcaína salt cod cooked with dried peppers, onions and parsley

bacalao al pil-pil a Basque speciality – salt cod cooked in a creamy garlic and olive oil sauce

bacalao con patatas salt cod slowly baked with potatoes, peppers, tomatoes, onions, olives and bay leaves
bandeja de quesos cheese platter
barbacoa, ...a la barbecued
berenjena aubergine (eggplant)
besugo red bream
bizcocho sponge
bizcocho borracho sponge soaked in wine and syrup
bocadillo sandwich (French bread)
bocadillo (de...) sandwich
bogavante lobster
bonito tunny fish, lighter than tuna, good grilled
boquerones fresh anchovies
boquerones en vinagre fresh anchovies marinated in garlic, parsley and olive oil
boquerones fritos fried anchovies
brasa, ...a la barbecued
buñuelos type of fritter. Savoury ones are filled with cheese, ham, mussels or prawns. Sweet ones can be filled with fruit
buñuelos de bacalao salt cod fritters
butifarra special sausage from Catalonia
butifarra blanca white sausage containing pork and tripe
butifarra negra black sausage containing pork blood, belly and spices

caballa mackerel
cabrito kid (goat)
cabrito al horno roast kid
café coffee
café con leche white coffee
café cortado coffee with only a little milk
café descafeinado decaffeinated coffee
café solo black coffee
calabacines courgettes
calabaza guisada stewed pumpkin
calamares squid
calamares en su tinta squid cooked in its own ink
calamares fritos fried squid
calamares rellenos stuffed squid
caldereta stew/casserole
caldo clear soup
caldo de pescado fish soup
caldo gallego clear soup with green vegetables, beans, pork and **chorizo**
caliente hot
callos tripe
camarones shrimps
cangrejo crab
caracoles snails
caracolillos winkles
carajillo black coffee with brandy which may be set alight depending on regional customs
carne meat
carne de buey beef

castaña chestnut
cazuela de fideos bean, meat and noodle stew
cebolla onion
cebollas rellenas stuffed onions
cebollas rojas red onions
centollo spider crab
cerdo pork
cerdo asado roast pork
cerezas cherries
champiñones mushrooms
chilindrón, ...al sauce made with pepper, tomato, fried onions and meat (pork or lamb)
chistorra spicy sausage from Navarra
chocolate either chocolate (for eating) or a hot thick drinking chocolate: **un chocolate**
chorizo spicy red sausage. The larger type is eaten like salami, the thinner type is cooked in various dishes
chuleta chop
chuletón large steak
churrasco barbecued steak
churros fried batter sticks sprinkled with sugar, usually eaten with thick hot chocolate; in some parts of Spain they are called **porras**
cigalas king prawns
ciruelas plums
coca (coques) type of pizza with meat, fish or vegetables served in the Balearic Islands.
cochinillo roast suckling pig

cocido stew made with various meats, vegetables and chickpeas. There are regional variations of this dish and it is worth trying the local version
coco coconut
cóctel de gambas prawn cocktail
codillo de cerdo pig's trotter
codorniz quail
col cabbage
coles de Bruselas Brussels sprouts
coliflor cauliflower
conejo rabbit
consomé consommé
copa de helado ice cream sundae
cordero lamb
costillas ribs
  costillas de cerdo pork ribs
crema cream soup/cream
  crema catalana similar to crème brûlée
croquetas croquettes (made with thick bechamel sauce)
crudo raw
cuajada cream-based dessert like junket, served with honey or sugar
cucurucho de helado ice cream cone

descafeinado decaffeinated
dorada sea bream
  dorada a la sal sea bream cooked in the oven, covered only with salt, forming a crust

dorada al horno baked sea bream
dulce sweet
dulces cakes and pastries

embutido sausage, cold meat
empanada pastry/pie filled with meat or fish and vegetables
empanadilla pasty/small pie filled with meat or fish
empanado breadcrumbed and fried
ensaimada sweet spiral-shaped yeast bun from Majorca
ensalada (mixta/verde) (mixed/green) salad
ensalada de la casa lettuce, tomato and onion salad (may include tuna)
ensaladilla rusa potato salad with diced vegetables, hard-boiled eggs and mayonnaise
entremeses starters
escabeche, ...en pickled
escalfado poached
escalivada salad of chargrilled or baked vegetables such as peppers and aubergines soaked in olive oil
escalope de ternera veal/beef escalope
escudella meat, vegetable and chickpea stew. Traditionally served as two courses: a soup and then the cooked meat and vegetables
espárragos asparagus
esqueixada salad made with salt cod
estofado braised/stewed

fabada asturiana pork, cured ham, black pudding, large butter beans or sausage stew with **chorizo** and **morcilla**
fiambre cold meat
fideos noodles/thin ribbons of pasta (vermicelli)
filete fillet steak
filete de ternera veal/beef steak
filetes de lenguado sole fillets
flan crème caramel
frambuesas raspberries
fresas strawberries
frito fried
fritura de pescado fried assortment of fish
fruta fruit
frutos secos nuts

galleta biscuit
gallina hen
gambas prawns
gambas a la plancha grilled prawns
gambas al ajillo grilled prawns with garlic
gambas al pil-pil sizzling prawns cooked with chillies
garbanzos chickpeas
gazpacho traditional cold tomato soup of southern Spain. There are many different recipes. Basic ingredients are water, tomatoes, garlic, fresh bread-crumbs, salt, vinegar and olive oil. Sometimes served with diced cucumber, hardboiled eggs and cured ham

gran reserva classification given to aged wines of exceptional quality
granada pomegranate
granizado/a fruit drink (usually lemon) with crushed ice
gratinado au gratin
grelos young turnip tops
guindilla chilli
guisado stew or casserole
guisantes peas
gulas a cheap alternative to **angulas**, made of fish (mainly haddock) and squid ink

habas broad beans
helado ice cream
hervido boiled
hígado liver
higos figs
horchata de chufas cool drink made with tiger (chufa) nuts
horno, ...al baked (in oven)
huevos eggs
  huevos a la flamenca baked eggs with tomatoes, peas, peppers, asparagus and **chorizo**

ibéricos traditional Spanish gourmet products; a **surtido de ibéricos** means assorted products such as cured ham, cheese, **chorizo** and **salchichón**
infusión herbal tea

jamón ham
jamón de Jabugo Andalusian prime-quality cured ham (from Jabugo, a small town in Huelva)
jamón serrano dark red cured ham
jamón (de) York cooked ham
judías beans
judías blancas haricot beans
judías verdes green beans
jurel horse mackerel

kokotxas hake's cheek, usually fried

lacón con grelos salted pork with young turnip tops and white cabbage
langosta lobster
langostinos king prawns
leche milk
leche frita very thick custard dipped into an egg and breadcrumb mixture, fried and served hot
lechuga lettuce
legumbres fresh or dried pulses
lengua tongue
lenguado sole
lentejas lentils (very popular in Spain)
limón lemon
lomo loin of pork
longaniza spicy pork sausage
lubina sea bass

macedonia de fruta fruit salad
maíz sweetcorn
manitas de cerdo pig's trotters
mantequilla butter
manzana apple
manzanilla camomile tea; also a very dry sherry from Sanlúcar de Barrameda
mariscada mixed shellfish
marisco shellfish ; seafood
marmitako tuna fish and potato stew
mazapán marzipan
medallón thick steak (medallion)
mejillones mussels
melocotón peach
melocotón en almíbar peaches in syrup
melón melon
menestra de verduras fresh vegetable stew often cooked with cured ham
merluza hake, one of the most popular fish in Spain
mermelada jam
mero grouper
miel honey
mojama cured tuna fish, a delicacy
mojo a sauce made from olive oil, vinegar, garlic and different spices. Paprika is added for the red **mojo**. Predominantly found in the Canaries
mojo picón spicy **mojo** made with chilli peppers
mojo verde made with fresh coriander
mollejas sweetbreads

morcilla black pudding
moros y cristianos rice, black beans and onions with garlic sausage
mostaza mustard
naranja orange
nata cream
natillas sort of custard
navajas razor clams
nécora sea crab
níspero medlar

olla stew made traditionally with white beans, beef and bacon
olla gitana thick stew/soup made with chickpeas, pork and vegetables and flavoured with almonds and saffron
olla podrida thick cured ham, vegetable and chickpea stew/soup
ostras oysters

paella one of the most famous of Spanish dishes. Paella varies from region to region but usually consists of rice, chicken, shellfish, vegetables, garlic and saffron. The traditional paella Valenciana contains rabbit, chicken and sometimes eel
pan bread
parrilla, ...a la grilled
pasas raisins
pastel cake/pastry

patatas potatoes
patatas bravas fried diced potatoes mixed with a garlic, oil and vinegar dressing and flavoured with tomatoes and red chilli peppers
patatas fritas chips/crisps
pato duck
pavo turkey
pechuga de pollo chicken breast
pepino cucumber
pepitoria de pavo/pollo turkey/chicken fricassée
pera pear
percebes goose-neck barnacles, a Galician shellfish
perdiz partridge
perejil parsley
pescado fish
pescaíto frito mixed fried fish
pez espada swordfish
pimienta pepper (spice)
pimientos red and green peppers
pimientos de piquillo pickled red peppers
pimientos morrones sweet red peppers
pimientos rellenos peppers stuffed with meat or fish
piña pineapple
pinchos small tapas
pinchos morunos pork grilled on a skewer. If you ask for a **pinchito** you can omit the word **moruno**, but if you say **pincho** you have to add **moruno**
plancha, ...a la grilled

plátano banana
pollo chicken
pollo al chilindrón chicken cooked with onion, ham, garlic, red pepper and tomatoes
pollo en pepitoria breaded chicken pieces casseroled with herbs, almonds, garlic and sherry
polvorones very crumbly cakes made with almonds and often eaten with a glass of **anís**
postres desserts
potaje thick soup/stew often with pork and pulses
pote thick soup with beans and sausage which has many regional variations
pote gallego thick soup made with cabbage, white kidney beans, potatoes, pork and sausage
puchero hotpot made from meat or fish
puchero canario salted fish and potatoes served with **mojo** sauce
puerros leeks
pulpo octopus
puré de patatas mashed potatoes

queimada warm drink made with **aguardiente** (pale brandy) sweetened with sugar and flamed, a speciality of Galicia
queso cheese
queso de oveja mild sheep's cheese from León
queso fresco soft fresh cheese

rabo de toro bull's tail, usually cooked in a stew
rape monkfish
rebozado in batter
rehogado lightly fried
relleno stuffed
revuelto scrambled eggs often cooked with another ingredient
riñones al jerez kidneys in sherry sauce
rodaballo turbot
romana, ...a la fried in batter (generally squid – **calamares**)
romesco sauce made traditionally with olive oil, red pepper and bread. Other ingredients are often added, such as almonds and garlic

sal salt
salchicha sausage
salchichón salami-type sausage
salmón salmon
  salmón ahumado smoked salmon
salmonete red mullet
salpicón chopped seafood or meat with tomato, onion, garlic and peppers
salsa sauce
  salsa verde garlic, olive oil and parsley sauce
salteado sautéed
sandía watermelon
sardinas sardines
sepia cuttlefish

sesos brains
setas wild mushrooms
sobrasada a paprika-flavoured pork sausage from Mallorca
sofrito basic sauce made with slowly fried onions, garlic and tomato
solomillo sirloin
sopa soup
sopa de ajo garlic soup with bread. May contain poached egg or cured ham
sorbete sorbet

tapas appetizers; snacks
tarta cake or tart
tarta helada ice-cream cake
té tea
ternera veal/beef
tocinillo (de cielo) dessert made with egg yolk and sugar
tocino bacon
tomates tomatoes
torrija bread dipped in milk and then fried and sprinkled with sugar and cinnamon
tortilla (española) traditional potato and onion omelette, often served as a tapa
trucha trout
turrón nougat
turrón de Alicante, turrón duro hard nougat
turrón de Jijona, turrón blando soft nougat

uvas grapes

vapor, ...al steamed
verduras vegetables
vieiras scallops
vinagre vinegar
yemas small cakes that look like egg yolks

zanahorias carrots
zarzuela de mariscos mixed seafood with wine and saffron
zarzuela de pescado fish stew
zumo juice
  zumo de melocotón peach juice
  zumo de naranja orange juice
  zumo de tomate tomato juice

Nouns

Unlike English, Spanish nouns have a gender: they are either masculine (**el**) or feminine (**la**). Therefore words for 'the' and 'a(n)' must agree with the noun they accompany – whether masculine, feminine or plural:

	masculine	feminine	plural
the	**el gato**	**la plaza**	**los gatos, las plazas**
a, an	**un gato**	**una plaza**	**unos gatos, unas plazas**

The ending of the noun will usually indicate whether it is masculine or feminine:

-**o** or -**or** are generally masculine
-**a**, -**dad**, -**ión**, -**tud**, -**umbre** are generally feminine

Formation of plurals

The articles **el** and **la** become **los** and **las** in the plural. Nouns ending with a vowel become plural by adding **-s**:

el gato → los gatos
la plaza → las plazas
la calle → las calles

If the noun ends in a consonant, **-es** is added:

el color → los colores
la ciudad → las ciudades

Nouns ending in **-z** change their ending to **-ces** in the plural:

el lápiz → los lápices
la voz → las voces

Grammar

Adjectives

Adjectives normally follow the nouns they describe in Spanish, e.g. **la manzana roja** (the red apple). Spanish adjectives also reflect the gender of the noun they describe. To make an adjective feminine, the masculine -**o** ending is changed to -**a**; and the endings -**án**, -**ón**, -**or**, -**és** change to -**ana**, -**ona**, -**ora**, -**esa** (adjectives ending in -**e** don't change):

masculine	feminine
el libro rojo (the red book)	**la manzana roja** (the red apple)
el hombre hablador (the talkative man)	**la mujer habladora** (the talkative woman)

To make an adjective plural an -**s** is added to the singular form if it ends in a vowel. If the adjective ends in a consonant, -**es** is added:

masculine	feminine
los libros rojos (the red books)	**las manzanas rojas** (the red apples)
los hombres habladores (the talkative men)	**las mujeres habladoras** (the talkative women)

My, your, his, her...

These words also depend on the gender and number of the noun they accompany and not on the sex of the 'owner'.

	with masc. sing. noun	with fem. sing. noun	with plural nouns
my	**mi**	**mi**	**mis**
your (familiar sing.)	**tu**	**tu**	**tus**
your (polite sing.)	**su**	**su**	**sus**
his/her/its	**su**	**su**	**sus**
our	**nuestro**	**nuestra**	**nuestros/ nuestras**
your (familiar pl.)	**vuestro**	**vuestra**	**vuestros/ vuestras**
your (polite pl.)	**su**	**su**	**sus**
their	**su**	**su**	**sus**

There is no distinction between 'his' and 'her' in Spanish: **su billete** can mean either his or her ticket.

Pronouns

A pronoun is a word that you use to refer to someone or something when you do not need to use a noun, often because the person or thing has been mentioned earlier. Examples are 'it', 'she', 'something' and 'myself'.

subject		**object**	
I	**yo**	me	**me**
you (familiar sing.)	**tú**	you	**te**
you (polite sing.)	**usted (Ud.)**	you	**le**
he/it	**él**	him/it	**le, lo**
she/it	**ella**	her/it	**le, la**
we (masc.) (fem.)	**nosotros** **nosotras**	us	**nos**
you (masc.) (fem.) (familiar pl.)	**vosotros** **vosotras**	you	**os**
you (polite pl.)	**ustedes (Uds.)**	you	**les**
they (masc.) (fem.)	**ellos** **ellas**	them them	**les, los** **les, las**

Subject pronouns (I, you, he, etc.) are generally omitted in Spanish, since the verb ending distinguishes the subject:

hablo	I speak
hablamos	we speak

Object pronouns are placed before the verb in Spanish:

la veo	I see her
los conocemos	we know them

However, in commands or requests they follow the verb:

¡ayúdame!	help me!
¡escúchale!	listen to him!

Except when they are expressed in the negative:

¡no me ayudes!	don't help me!
¡no le escuches!	don't listen to him!

The object pronouns shown above can be used to mean 'to me', 'to us', etc., but 'to him/to her' is **le** and 'to them' is **les**. If **le** and **les** occur in combinations with **lo/la/las/los** then **le/les** change to **se**, e.g. **se lo doy** (I give it to him).

Verbs

A verb is a word such as 'sing', 'walk' or 'cry' which is used with a subject to say what someone or something does or what happens to them. Regular verbs follow the same pattern of endings. Irregular verbs do not follow a regular pattern so you need to learn the different endings.

There are three main patterns of endings for Spanish verbs – those ending -**ar**, -**er** and -**ir** in the dictionary.

	cantar	**to sing**
	canto	I sing
	cantas	you sing
(usted)	**canta**	(s)he sings/you sing
	cantamos	we sing
	cantáis	you sing
(ustedes)	**cantan**	they sing/you sing

	vivir	**to live**
	vivo	I live
	vives	you live
(usted)	**vive**	(s)he lives/you live
	vivimos	we live
	vivís	you live
(ustedes)	**viven**	they live/you live

	comer	**to eat**
	como	I eat
	comes	you eat
(usted)	**come**	(s)he eats/you eat
	comemos	we eat
	coméis	you eat
(ustedes)	**comen**	they eat/you eat

In Spanish there are two ways of addressing people: the polite form (for people you don't know well or who are older) and the familiar form (for friends, family and children). The polite you is **usted** in the singular, and **ustedes** in the plural. You can see from above that **usted** uses the same verb ending as for he and she; **ustedes** the same ending as for they. Often the words **usted** and **ustedes** are omitted, but the verb ending itself indicates that you are using the polite form. The informal words for you are **tú** (singular) and **vosotros/as** (plural).

The verb 'to be'

There are two different Spanish verbs for 'to be' – **ser** and **estar**.

Ser is used to describe a permanent state:

soy inglés	I am English
es una playa	it is a beach

Estar is used to describe a temporary state or where something is located:

¿cómo está?	how are you?
¿dónde está la playa?	where is the beach?

	ser	**to be**
	soy	I am
	eres	you are
(usted)	**es**	(s)he is/you are
	somos	we are
	sois	you are
(ustedes)	**son**	they are/you are

	estar	**to be**
	estoy	I am
	estás	you are
(usted)	**está**	(s)he is/you are
	estamos	we are
	estáis	you are
(ustedes)	**están**	they are/you are

Other common irregular verbs include:

	tener	**to have**
	tengo	I have
	tienes	you have
(usted)	**tiene**	(s)he has/you have
	tenemos	we have
	tenéis	you have
(ustedes)	**tienen**	they have/you have

	ir	**to go**
	voy	I go
	vas	you go
(usted)	**va**	(s)he goes/you go
	vamos	we go
	vais	you go
(ustedes)	**van**	they go/you go

	querer	**to want**
	quiero	I want
	quieres	you want
(usted)	**quiere**	(s)he wants/you want
	queremos	we want
	queréis	you want
(ustedes)	**quieren**	they want/you want

	hacer	**to do**
	hago	I do
	haces	you do
(usted)	**hace**	(s)he does/you do
	hacemos	we do
	hacéis	you do
(ustedes)	**hacen**	they do/you do

Public holidays

January 1	**Año Nuevo** New Year's Day
January 6	**Día de Reyes** Epiphany or the Adoration of the Magi
March 19	**San José/el Día del Padre** Father's Day
May 1	**Día del Trabajo** Labour Day
August 15	**La Asunción** Assumption Day
October 12	**Día de la Hispanidad** Spain's National Day
November 1	**Día de Todos los Santos** All Saints' Day
December 6	**Día de la Constitución** Constitution Day
December 8	**Día de la Inmaculada** Inmaculate Conception
December 25	**Día de Navidad** Christmas Day
Variable	**Jueves y Viernes Santo** Maundy Thursday and Good Friday

As well as the above national holidays, each town celebrates the feast-day of its patron saint, which differs from town to town.

English – Spanish

A

a(n)	un(a)	oon/**oo**na
about (concerning)	sobre	**so**-bre
above	arriba; por encima	a-**rree**-ba; por en-**thee**-ma
abroad	en el extranjero	en el eks-tran-**khe**-ro
access	el acceso	ak-**the**-so
wheelchair access	el acceso para sillas de ruedas	
accident	el accidente	ak-thee-**den**-te
accommodation	el a-lojamiento	el a-lo-kha-**myen**-to
account (bank, etc)	la cuenta	**kwen**ta
account number	el número de cuenta	**noo**-me-ro de **kwen**ta
to ache	doler	do-**lair**
my head aches	me duele la cabeza	
admission charge/fee	el precio de entrada	**pre**-thyo de en-**tra**-da
adult	el/la adulto(a)	a-**dool**-to(a)
advance:		
in advance	por adelantado	por a-de-lan-**ta**-do
A&E	las urgencias	oor-**khen**-thyas
after	después	des**pwes**
afternoon	la tarde	**tar**de
this afternoon	esta tarde	
in the afternoon	por la tarde	
again	otra vez	**o**-tra beth
age	la edad	e-**dad**
ago:		
a week ago	hace una semana	**a**-the **oo**na se-**ma**-na
air conditioning	el aire acondicionado	**aee**-re a-kon-dee-thyo-**na**-do
airplane	el avión	a-**byon**

airport bus	el autobús del aeropuerto	ow-to-**boos** del a-e-ro-**pwair**-to
air ticket	el billete de avión	bee-**lye**-te de a-**byon**
alarm	la alarma	a-**lar**-ma
alarm clock	el despertador	des-pair-ta-**dor**
alcohol	el alcohol	al**kol**
alcohol-free	sin alcohol	seen al**kol**
all	todo(a)/ todos(as)	**to**-do(a)/ **to**-dos(as)
allergic to	alérgico(a) a	a-**lair**-khee-ko(a) a
I'm allergic to...	soy alérgico(a) a...	
allergy	la alergia	a-**lair**-khya
all right (agreed)	de acuerdo	de a-**kwair**-do
(OK)	vale	**ba**-le
are you all right?	¿está bien?	
alone	solo(a)	**so**-lo(a)
already	ya	ya
also	también	tam**byen**
always	siempre	**syem**pre

a.m.	de la mañana	de la ma-**nya**-na
ambulance	la ambulancia	am-boo-**lan**-thya
America	Norteamérica	nor-te-a-**me**-ree-ka
American	norte americano(a)	nor-te-a-me-ree-**ka**-no(a)
anaesthetic	la anestesia	a-nes-**te**-sya
and	y	ee
angina	la angina (de pecho)	an-**khee**-na (de **pe**-cho)
angry	enfadado(a)	en-fa-**da**-do(a)
another	otro(a)	**o**-tro(a)
answer	la respuesta	res-**pwes**-ta
to answer	responder	res-pon-**dair**
antibiotic	el antibiótico	an-tee-**byo**-tee-ko
antihistamine	el antihistamínico	an-tee-eesta-**mee**-nee-ko
antiseptic	el antiséptico	an-tee-**sep**-tee-ko
any	alguno(a)	al-**goo**-no(a)
anyone	alguien	**al**gyen

English – Spanish

anything	algo	**al**go
apartment	el apartamento	a-par-ta-**men**-to
apple	la manzana	man-**tha**-na
apricot	el albaricoque	al-ba-ree-**ko**-ke
April	abril	a**breel**
arm	el brazo	**bra**-tho
to arrest	detener	de-te-**nair**
arrivals (plane, train)	las llegadas	lye-**ga**-das
to arrive	llegar	lye-**gar**
art	el arte	**ar**te
to ask (question)	preguntar	pre-goon-**tar**
(ask for something)	pedir	pe-**deer**
aspirin	la aspirina	as-pee-**ree**-na
asthma	el asma	**as**ma
I have asthma	tengo asma	
at	a; en	a; en
at home	en casa	en **ka**-sa
at 8 o'clock	a las ocho	
at night	por la noche	
to attack	atacar	a-ta-**kar**

August	agosto	a-**gos**-to
Australia	Australia	ows-**tra**-lya
Australian	australiano(a)	ows-tra-**lya**-no(a)
autumn	el otoño	o-**to**-nyo
available	disponible	dees-po-**nee**-ble
away: *far away*	lejos	**le**-khos

B

baby	el bebé	be-**be**
baby food	los potitos	po-**tee**-tos
baby milk	la leche infantil	**le**-che een-fan-**teel**
babyseat (in car)	el asiento del bebé	a-**syen**-to del be-**be**
baby wipes	las toallitas infantiles	twa-**lyee**-tas een-fan-**tee**-les
back (of body)	la espalda	es-**pal**-da
bad (weather, news)	mal/malo(a)	mal/**ma**-lo(a)
(fruit and veg.)	podrido(a)	po-**dree**-do(a)
bag	la bolsa	**bol**

baggage	el equipaje	e-kee-**pa**-khe
baker's	la panadería	pa-na-de-**ree**-a
banana	el plátano	**pla**-ta-no
bank	el banco	**ban**ko
bank account	la cuenta bancaria	**kwen**ta ban-**ka**-rya
banknote	el billete	bee-**lye**-te
bar	el bar	bar
bath	el baño	**ba**-nyo
bathroom	el cuarto de baño	**kwar**to de **ba**-nyo
battery (radio,	la pila	**pee**la
(in car)	la batería	ba-te-**ree**-a
B&B (guesthouse)	la pensión	pen**syon**
to be	estar; ser	es**tar**; sair
beach	la playa	**pla**-ya
beautiful	hermoso(a)	air-**mo**-so(a)
because	porque	**por**ke
bed	la cama	**ka**-ma
bed and breakfast	alojamiento y desayuno	a-lo-kha-**myen**-to ee de-sa-**yoo**-no

bedroom	el dormitorio	dor-mee-**to**-ryo
beer	la cerveza	thair-**be**-tha
before	antes de	**an**tes de
to begin	empezar	em-pe-**thar**
behind	detrás de	de-**tras** de
below	debajo; por debajo	de-**ba**-kho; por de-**ba**-kho
beside (next to)	al lado de	al **la**-do de
beside the bank	al lado del banco	
best	el/la mejor	me-**khor**
better	mejor	me-**khor**
better than	mejor que	
between	entre	**en**tre
bicycle	la bicicleta	bee-thee-**kle**-ta
by bicycle	en bicicleta	
big	grande	**gran**de
bigger than	mayor que	
bill	la factura	fak-**too**-ra
(in restaurant)	la cuenta	**kwen**ta
birthday	el cumpleaños	koom-ple-**a**-nyos
biscuits	las galletas	ga-**lye**-tas

English – Spanish

bit: ***a bit of***	un poco de	oon **po**-ko de
bite (insect)	la picadura	pee-ka-**doo**-ra
(animal)	la mordedura	mor-de-**doo**-ra
black	negro(a)	**ne**-gro(a)
to bleed	sangrar	san**grar**
blind (person)	ciego(a)	**thye**-go(a)
blond (person)	rubio(a)	**roo**byo(a)
blood	la sangre	**san**gre
blood group	el grupo sanguíneo	**groo**po san-**gee**-ne-o
blood pressure	la presión sanguínea	pre-**syon** san-**gee**-ne-a
blood test	el análisis de sangre	a-**na**-lee-sees de **san**gre
blouse	la blusa	**bloo**sa
blue	azul	a-**thool**
to board (train, etc)	subir	soo**beer**
boarding card/ pass	la tarjeta de embarque	tar-**khe**-ta de em-**bar**-ke
body	el cuerpo	**kwair**po
to boil	hervir	air**beer**

book	el libro	**lee**bro
to book	reservar	re-sair-**bar**
booking	la reserva	re-**sair**-ba
booking office (train)	la ventanilla de billetes	ben-ta-**nee**-lya de bee-**lye**-tes
bookshop	la librería	lee-bre-**ree**-a
boots	las botas	**bo**-tas
both	ambos(as)	**am**bos(as)
bottle	la botella	bo-**te**-lya
bottle opener	el abrebotellas	a-bre-bo-**te**-lyas
box office	la taquilla	ta-**kee**-lya
boy	el chico	**chee**ko
boyfriend	el novio	**no**-byo
brake	el freno	**fre**-no
to brake	frenar	fre-**nar**
brand (make)	la marca	**mar**ka
bread	el pan	pan
to break	romper	rom**pair**
breakfast	el desayuno	desa-**yoo**-no
breast	el pecho	**pe**-cho
bride	la novia	

bridegroom	el novio	**no**-byo
briefcase	la cartera	kar-**tair**-a
to bring	traer	tra-**air**
Britain	Gran Bretaña	gran bre-**ta**-nya
British	británico(a)	bree-**tan**-ee-ko(a)
brochure	el folleto	fo-**lye**-to
broken	roto(a)	**ro**-to(a)
broken down (car, etc)	averiado(a)	a-be-**rya**-do(a)
bronchitis	la bronquitis	bron-**kee**-tees
brother	el hermano	air-**ma**-no
brown	marrón	ma-**rron**
buffet car	el coche comedor	**ko**-che ko-me-**dor**
to build	construir	kons-troo-**eer**
bulb (electric)	la bombilla	bom-**bee**-lya
bureau de change	la oficina de cambio	o-fee-**thee**-na de **kam**-byo
burger	la hamburguesa	am-boor-**ge**-sa
bus	el autobús	ow-to-**boos**
bus pass	el bonobús	bo-no-**boos**
bus station	la estación de autobuses	es-ta-**thyon** de ow-to-**boo**-ses
bus stop	la parada de autobús	pa-**ra**-da de ow-to-**boos**
bus ticket	el billete de autobús	bee-**lye**-te de ow-to-**boos**
business	el negocio	ne-**go**-thyo
on business	de negocios	
businessman/ woman	el hombre/ la mujer de negocios	**om**bre/ moo**khair** de ne-**go**-thyos
business trip	el viaje de negocios	**bya**-khe de ne-**go**-thyos
busy	ocupado(a)	o-koo-**pa**-do(a)
but	pero	**pe**-ro
butcher's	la carnicería	kar-nee-the-**ree**-a
butter	la mantequilla	man-te-**kee**-lya
to buy	comprar	kom**prar**
by (via)	por	por
(beside)	al lado de	al **la**-do de
by air	en avión	

by bus	en autobús	
by car	en coche	
by train	en tren	
by ship	en barco	

C

café	el café	ka-**fe**
cake	el pastel	pas**tel**
call (telephone)	la llamada	lya-**ma**-da
to call	llamar	lya-**mar**
(phone)	llamar por teléfono	lya-**mar** por te-**le**-fo-no
camcorder	la videocámara	bee-de-o-**ka** ma-ra
camera	la cámara	**ka**-ma-ra
to camp	acampar	a-kam-**par**
campsite	el camping	**kam**peen
can (to be able)	poder	po-**dair**
Canada	(el) Canadá	ka-na-**da**
Canadian	canadiense	ka-na-**dyen**-se
to cancel	anular; cancelar	a-noo-**lar**; kan-the-**lar**
cancellation	la cancelación	kan-the-la-**thyon**
car	el coche	**ko**-che
car alarm	la alarma de coche	a-**lar**-ma de **ko**-che
car hire	el alquiler de coches	al-kee-**lair** de **ko**-ches
car insurance	el seguro del coche	se-**goo**-ro del **ko**-che
car keys	las llaves del coche	**lya**-bes del **ko**-che
car park	el aparcamiento	a-par-ka-**myen**-to
card (greetings, business)	la tarjeta	tar-**khe**-ta
to carry	llevar	lye-**bar**
case (suitcase)	la maleta	ma-**le**-ta
cash	el dinero en efectivo	dee-**ne**-ro en e-fek-**tee**-bo
to cash (cheque)	cobrar	ko-**brar**
cash desk	la caja	**ka**-kha
cash dispenser	el cajero automático	ka-**khe**-ro ow-to-**ma**-tee-ko

cashier	el/la cajero(a)	ka-**khe**-ro(a)
castle	el castillo	kas-**tee**-lyo
cat	el gato	**ga**-to
to catch (bus, etc)	coger	ko-**khair**
cathedral	la catedral	ka-te-**dral**
Catholic	católico(a)	ka-**to**-lee-ko(a)
cent	el céntimo	**then**-tee-mo
central	central	then**tral**
central heating	la calefacción central	ka-le-fak-**thyon** then**tral**
centre	el centro	**then**tro
cereal	los cereales	the-re-**a**-les
chair	la silla	**see**lya
chalet	el chalet	cha-**let**
change	el cambio	**kam**byo
(small coins)	el suelto	**swel**to
(money returned)	la vuelta	**bwel**ta
to change	cambiar	kam**byar**
(clothes)	cambiarse	kam-**byar**-se
(train)	hacer transbordo	a-**thair** trans-**bor**-do
to change money	cambiar dinero	
charge (fee)	el precio	**pre**-thyo
(electrical)	la carga	**kar**ga
to charge (money)	cobrar	ko-**brar**
(battery)	cargar	kar**gar**
cheap	barato(a)	ba-**ra**-to(a)
to check	revisar; comprobar	re-bee-**sar**; kom-pro-**bar**
to check in (at airport)	facturar el equipaje	fak-too-**rar** e-kee-**pa**-khe
(at hotel)	registrarse	re-khees-**trar**-se
check-in	la facturación	fak-too-ra-**thyon**
cheers!	¡salud!	¡sa-**lood**!
cheese	el queso	**ke**-so
chef	el chef	chef
chemist's	la farmacia	far-**ma**-thya
cheque	el cheque	**che**-ke
cheque book	el talonario	ta-lo-**na**-ryo
cherry	la cereza	the-**re**-tha
chicken	el pollo	**po**-lyo
child boy/girl	el niño/la niña	**nee**nyo/ **nee**nya

children (infants)	los niños	**nee**nyos
chips	las patatas fritas	pa-**ta**-tas **free**tas
chocolate	el chocolate	cho-ko-**la**-te
chocolates	los bombones	bom-**bo**-nes
Christmas	la Navidad	na-bee-**dad**
Christmas Eve	la Nochebuena	no-che-**bwe**-na
church	la iglesia	ee-**gle**-sya
cigarette	el cigarrillo	thee-ga-**rree**-lyo
cigarette lighter	el mechero	me-**che**-ro
cinema	el cine	**thee**ne
city	la ciudad	thyoo**dad**
city centre	el centro de la ciudad	**then**tro de la thyoo**dad**
class: ***first class***	primera clase	
second class	segunda clase	
clean	limpio(a)	**leem**pyo(a)
to clean	limpiar	leem**pyar**
clear	claro(a)	**kla**-ro(a)
client	el/la client(a)	klee-**en**-te(a)

clock	el reloj	re-**lokh**
to close	cerrar	the-**rrar**
closed (shop, etc)	cerrado(a)	the-**rra**-do(a)
clothes	la ropa	**ro**-pa
clothes shop	la tienda de ropa	**tyen**da de **ro**-pa
cloudy	nublado(a)	noo-**bla**-do(a)
coach (bus)	el autocar	ow-to-**kar**
coast	la costa	**kos**ta
coat	el abrigo	a-**bree**-go
coffee	el café	ka-**fe**
coin	la moneda	mo-**ne**-da
cold	frío(a)	**free**-o(a)
I'm cold	tengo frío	
it's cold	hace frío	
cold (illness)	el resfriado	res-free-**a**-do
I have a cold	estoy resfriado(a)	
to come	venir	be-**neer**
(to arrive)	llegar	lye-**gar**
to come back	volver	bol**bair**
to come in	entrar	en**trar**
come in!	¡pase!	

comfortable	cómodo(a)	**ko**-mo-do(a)
company (firm)	la empresa	em-**pre**-sa
to complain	reclamar	re-kla-**mar**
complaint	la reclamación; la queja	re-kla-ma-**thyon**; **ke**-kha
computer	el ordenador	or-de-na-**dor**
concert	el concierto	kon-**thyair**-to
concert hall	la sala de conciertos	**sa**-la de kon-**thyair**-tos
conditioner	el suavizante	swa-bee-**than**-te
condom	el condón	kon**don**
conductor (on bus)	el/la cobrador(a)	ko-bra-**dor**(a)
(on train)	el/la revisor(a)	re-bee-**sor**(a)
conference	el congreso	kon-**gre**-so
to confirm	confirmar	kon-feer-**mar**
confirmation (flight, booking)	la confirmación	kon-feer-ma-**thyon**
connection	el enlace	en-**la**-the
consulate	el consulado	kon-soo-**la**-do
to contact	ponerse en contacto con	po-**nair**-se en kon-**tak**-tc kon
contact lens	la lentilla	len-**tee**-lya
to continue	continuar	kon-tee-**nwar**
contraceptive	el anticonceptivo	an-tee-kon-thep-**tee**-bo
contract	el contrato	kon-**tra**-to
to cook	cocinar	ko-thee-**nar**
cooked	preparado(a)	pre-pa-**ra**-do(a)
cooker	la cocina	ko-**thee**-na
corner	la esquina	es-**kee**-na
corridor	el pasillo	pa-**see**-lyo
cosmetics	los cosméticos	kos-**me**-tee-kos
cost (price)	el precio	**pre**-thyo
to cost	costar	kos**tar**
how much does it cost?	¿cuánto cuesta?	
costume (swim.)	el bañador	ba-nya-**dor**
cough	la tos	tos
to cough	toser	to-**sair**
country (nation)	el país	pa-**ees**
couple (2 people)	la pareja	pa-**re**-kha
course (of study)	el curso	**koor**so

(of meal) el plato **pla**-to
cover charge (in restaurant) el cubierto koo-**byair**-to
crafts la artesanía ar-te-sa-**nee**-a
crash (car) el accidente ak-thee-**den**-te
cream (lotion) la crema **kre**-ma
(on milk) la nata **na**-ta
credit card la tarjeta de crédito tar-**khe**-ta de **kre**-dee-to
crisps las patatas fritas pa-**ta**-tas **free**tas
to cross (road) cruzar kroo**thar**
crossroads el cruce **kroo**the
to cry (weep) llorar lyo-**rar**
cup la taza **ta**-tha
customer el/la cliente(a) klee-**en**-te(a)
customs (control) la aduana a-doo-**a**-na
to cut cortar kor**tar**
to cycle ir en bicicleta eer en bee-thee-**kle**-ta
cystitis la cistitis thees-**tee**-tees

D

daily (each day) cada día; diario **ka**-da **dee**-a; dee-**a**-ryo
dairy produce los productos lácteos pro-**dook**-tos **lak**-te-os
damage el/los daño(s) **da**-nyo(s)
danger el peligro pe-**lee**-gro
dangerous peligroso(a) pe-lee-**gro**-so(a)
dark oscuro(a) os-**koo**-ro(a)
date la fecha **fe**-cha
date of birth la fecha de nacimiento **fe**-cha de na-thee-**myen**-to
daughter la hija **ee**kha
day el día **dee**-a
every day todos los días
deaf sordo(a) **sor**do(a)
debt la deuda **deoo**-da
debit card la tarjeta de débito tar-**khe**-ta de **de**-bee-to
December diciembre dee-**thyem**-bre
to declare declarar de-kla-**rar**

nothing to declare	nada que declarar	
deep	profundo(a)	pro-**foon**-do(a)
delay	el retraso	re-**tra**-so
delayed	retrasado(a)	re-tra-**sa**-do(a)
dentist	el/la dentista	den-**tees**-ta
deodorant	el desodorante	de-so-do-**ran**-te
department (gen)	el departamento	de-par-ta-**men**-to
(in shop)	la sección	sek**thyon**
department store	los grandes almacenes	**gran**des al-ma-**the**-nes
departure lounge	la sala de embarque	**sa**-la de em-**bar**-ke
dessert	el postre	**pos**tre
details	los detalles	de-**ta**-lyes
(personal)	los datos personales	**da**-tos pair-so-**na**-les
to develop (photos)	revelar	re-be-**lar**
diabetic	diabético(a)	dya-**be**-tee-ko(a)
I'm diabetic	soy diabético(a)	
to dial	marcar	mar**kar**
dialling code	el prefijo	pre-**fee**-kho
dialling tone	el tono de marcado	**to**-no de mar-**ka**-do
diesel	el diesel; el gasóleo; el gasoil	**dye**-sel; ga-**so**-le-o; ga-**soyl**
diet	la dieta	**dye**-ta
I'm on a diet	estoy a dieta	
different	distinto(a)	dees-**teen**-to(a)
difficult	difícil	dee-**fee**-theel
digital camera	la cámara digital	**ka**-ma-ra dee-khee-**tal**
dining room	el comedor	ko-me-**dor**
dinner (evening meal)	la cena	**the**-na
to have dinner	cenar	
direct (train, etc)	directo(a)	dee-**rek**-to(a)
directions (instructions)	las instrucciones	een-strook-**thyo**-nes

to ask for directions	preguntar el camino	
directory (phone)	la guía telefónica	**gee**-a te-le-**fo**-nee-ka
dirty	sucio(a)	**soo**thyo(a)
disabled	discapacitado(a)	dees-ka-pa-thee-**ta**-do(a)
disco	la discoteca	dees-ko-**te**-ka
discount	el descuento	des-**kwen**-to
to discover	descubrir	des-koo-**breer**
disease	la enfermedad	en-fair-me-**dad**
distance	la distancia	dees-**tan**-thya
district	el barrio	**ba**-rryo
diversion	el desvío	des-**bee**-o
divorced	divorciado(a)	dee-bor-**thya**-do(a)
dizzy	mareado(a)	ma-re-**a**-do(a)
to do	hacer	a-**thair**
doctor	el/la médico(a)	**me**-dee-ko(a)
documents	los documentos	do-koo-**men**-tos
dog	el perro	**pe**-rro
dollar	el dólar	**do**-lar
door	la puerta	**pwair**ta
double	doble	**do**-ble
double room	la habitación doble	a-bee-ta-**thyon** **do**-ble
down:		
to go down	bajar	ba-**khar**
downstairs	abajo	a-**ba**-kho
draught lager	la cerveza de barril	thair-**be**-tha de ba-**rreel**
dress	el vestido	bes-**tee**-do
drink	la bebida	be-**bee**-da
to drink	beber	be-**bair**
drinking water	el agua potable	**a**-gwa po-**ta**-ble
to drive	conducir	kon-doo-**theer**
driver	el/la conductor(a)	kon-dook-**tor**(a)
driving licence	el carné de conducir	kar-**ne** de kon-doo-**theer**
to drown	ahogarse	a-o-**gar**-se
drug	la droga	**dro**-ga
(medicine)	la medicina	me-dee-**thee**-na

drunk	borracho(a)	bo-**rra**-cho(a)
dry	seco(a)	**se**-ko(a)
to dry	secar	se-**kar**
during	durante	doo-**ran**-te
duty-free	libre de impuestos	**lee**bre de eem-**pwes**-tos
DVD player	el reproductor de DVD	re-pro-dook-**tor** de de-**oo**be-**de**

E

ear (outside)	la oreja	o-**re**-kha
(inside)	el oído	o-**ee**-do
earache	el dolor de oído(s)	do-**lor** de o-**ee**-do(s)
earlier	antes	**an**tes
early	temprano	tem-**pra**-no
to earn	ganar	ga-**nar**
east	el este	**es**te
Easter	la Pascua; la Semana Santa	**pas**-kwa; se-**ma**-na **san**ta
easy	fácil	**fa**-theel
to eat	comer	ko-**mair**
egg	el huevo	**we**-bo
elastoplast®	la tirita	tee-**ree**-ta
electric	eléctrico(a)	e-**lek**-tree-ko(a)
electrician	el/la electricista	e-lek-tree-**thees**-ta
electricity	la electricidad	e-lek-tree-thee-**dad**
electronic	electrónico(a)	e-lek-**tro**-nee-ko(a)
e-mail	el email	ee**meyl**
e-mail address	el email	ee**meyl**
embassy	la embajada	em-ba-**kha**-da
emergency	la emergencia	e-mair-**khen**-thya
emergency exit	la salida de emergencia	sa-**lee**-da de e-mair-**khen**-thya
empty	vacío(a)	ba-**thee**-o(a)
end	el fin	feen
engaged (to marry)	prometido(a)	pro-me-**tee**-do(a)
(toilet, phone)	ocupado(a)	o-koo-**pa**-do(a)
England	Inglaterra	een-gla-**te**-rra

English	inglés/inglesa	een**gles**/ een-**gle**-sa
(language)	el inglés	een**gles**
to enjoy (to like)	gustar	goos**tar**
enjoy your meal!	¡qué aproveche!	
enough	bastante	bas-**tan**-te
enquiry desk	la información	een-for-ma-**thyon**
to enter	entrar en	en**trar** en
entrance	la entrada	en-**tra**-da
entrance fee	el precio de entrada	**pre**-thyo de la en-**tra**-da
to escape	escapar	es-ka-**par**
euro	el euro	**eoo**-ro
Europe	Europa	eoo-**ro**-pa
European	el/la europeo(a)	eoo-ro-**pe**-o(a)
European Union	la Unión Europea	oo**nyon** eoo-ro-**pe**-a
evening	la tarde	**tar**de
every	cada	**ka**-da
everyone	todo el mundo; todos	**to**-do el **moon**do; **to**-dos
everything	todo	**to**-do
everywhere	en todas partes	en **to**-das **par**tes
example:		
for example	por ejemplo	por e-**khem**-plo
excellent	excelente	eks-the-**len**-te
to exchange	cambiar	kam**byar**
exchange rate	el tipo de cambio	**tee**po de **kam**byo
excuse:		
excuse me!	¡perdón!	¡pair**don**!
exercise	el ejercicio	e-khair-**thee**-thyo
exit	la salida	sa-**lee**-da
expensive	caro(a)	**ka**-ro(a)
to expire (ticket, etc)	caducar	ka-doo-**kar**
to explain	explicar	eks-plee-**kar**
to export	exportar	eks-por-**tar**
extra (in addition)	de más	de **mas**
(more)	extra	**eks**tra
eye	el ojo	**o**-kho

F

face	la cara	**ka**-ra
facilities	las instalaciones	eens-ta-la-**thyo**-nes
to faint	desmayarse	des-ma-**yar**-se
fair (hair)	rubio(a)	**roo**byo(a)
(just)	justo(a)	**khoo**sto(a)
fake	falso(a)	**fal**so(a)
to fall	caer; caerse	ka-**air**; ka-**air**-se
family	la familia	fa-**mee**-lya
famous	famoso(a)	fa-**mo**-so(a)
fan (electric)	el ventilador	ben-tee-la-**dor**
(hand-held)	el abanico	a-ba-**nee**-ko
far	lejos	**le**-khos
fast	rápido(a)	**ra**-pee-do(a)
to fasten	abrocharse	a-bro-**char**-se
fat (plump)	gordo(a)	**gor**do(a)
(in food, on person)	la grasa	**gra**-sa
father	el padre	**pa**-dre
fault (defect)	el defecto	de-**fek**-to
favour	el favor	fa-**bor**
fax	el fax	faks
by fax	por fax	
to fax	mandar por fax	man**dar** por faks
February	febrero	fe-**bre**-ro
to feed	dar de comer	dar de ko-**mair**
to feel	sentir	sen**teer**
I don't feel well	no me siento bien	
female	mujer	moo**khair**
fever	la fiebre	**fye**-bre
few	pocos(as)	**po**-kos(as)
a few	algunos(as)	
to fill	llenar	lye-**nar**
to fill in (form)	rellenar	re-lye-**nar**
fillet	el filete	fee-**le**-te
film (at cinema)	la película	pe-**lee**-koo-la
(for camera)	el carrete	ka-**rre**-te
to find	encontrar	en-kon-**trar**
fine (to be paid)	la multa	**mool**ta
finger	el dedo	**de**-do
to finish	acabar	a-ka-**bar**

finished	terminado(a)	tair-mee-**na**-do(a)
fire (flames)	el fuego	**fwe**-go
(blaze)	el incendio	een-**then**-dyo
fire!	¡fuego!	
fire alarm	la alarma de incendios	a-**lar**-ma de een-**then**-dyos
fire exit	la salida de incendios	sa-**lee**-da de een-**then**-dyos
firm (company)	la empresa	em-**pre**-sa
first	primero(a)	pree-**me**-ro(a)
first aid	los primeros auxilios	pree-**me**-ros ow-**see**-lyos
first class	de primera clase	de pree-**mair**-a **kla**-se
first name	el nombre de pila	**nom**-bre de **pee**-la
fish (food)	el pescado	pes-**ka**-do
(alive)	el pez	peth
to fish	pescar	pes-**kar**
fit (seizure)	el ataque	a-**ta**-ke
to fit (clothes)	quedar bien	ke-**dar** byen

to fix	arreglar	a-rre-**glar**
can you fix it?	¿puede arreglarlo?	
fizzy	con gas	kon gas
flat (apartment)	el piso	**pee**so
flat	llano(a)	**lya**-no(a)
(battery)	descargado(a)	des-kar-**ga**-do(a)
flavour	el sabor	sa-**bor**
flight	el vuelo	**bwe**-lo
floor (of building)	el piso	**pee**so
(of room)	el suelo	**swe**-lo
flower	la flor	flor
flu	la gripe	**gree**pe
to fly	volar	bo-**lar**
fog	la niebla	**nye**-bla
to fold	doblar	do-**blar**
to follow	seguir	se-**geer**
food	la comida	ko-**mee**-da
food poisoning	la intoxicación por alimentos	een-tok-see-ka-**thyon** por a-lee-**men**-tos
foot	el pie	pye

on foot	a pie	
for	para; por	**pa**ra; por
forbidden	prohibido(a)	pro-ee-**bee**-do(a)
foreigner	el/la extranjero(a)	eks-tran-**khe**-ro(a)
forever	para siempre	pa-ra **syem**-pre
to forget	olvidar	ol-bee-**dar**
fork (for eating)	el tenedor	te-ne-**dor**
form (document)	el impreso	eem-**pre**-so
fortnight	quince días	**keen**the **dee**-as
forward	adelante	a-de-**lan**-te
fountain	la fuente	**fwen**te
fracture	la fractura	frak-**tu**-ra
free (not occupied)	libre	**lee**bre
(costing nothing)	gratis	**gra**-tees
fresh	fresco(a)	**fres**ko(a)
Friday	el viernes	**byair**nes
fried	frito(a)	**free**to(a)
friend	el/la amigo(a)	a-**mee**-go(a)
from	de; desde	de; **des**de
from Scotland	de Escocia	
from England	de Inglaterra	
front	la parte delantera	**par**te de-lan-**te**-ra
in front of	delante de	
fruit	la fruta	**froo**ta
to fry	freir	fre-**eer**
fuel (petrol)	la gasolina	ga-so-**lee**-na
full	lleno(a)	**lye**-no(a)
(occupied)	ocupado(a)	o-koo-**pa**-do(a)
full board	pensión completa	pen**syon** kom-**ple**-ta
furnished	amueblado(a)	a-mwe-**bla**-do(a)

G

game	el juego	**khwe**-go
(animal)	la caza	**ka**-tha
garage	el garaje	ga-**ra**-khe
(for repairs)	el taller	ta-**lyair**
(for petrol)	la gasolinera	ga-so-lee-**ne**-ra
garden	el jardín	khar**deen**
gate (airport)	la puerta	**pwair**ta

gay (person)	gay	gey
gents (toilet)	los servicios de caballeros	sair-**bee**-thyos de ka-ba-**lye**-ros
to get (to obtain)	conseguir	kon-se-**geer**
(to receive)	recibir	re-thee-**beer**
(to bring)	traer	tra-**air**
to get in/on	subir (al)	soo**beer** (al)
to get out/off	bajarse de	ba-**khar**-se de
gift	el regalo	re-**ga**-lo
gift shop	la tienda de regalos	**tyen**da de re-**ga**-los
girl	la chica	**chee**ka
girlfriend	la novia	**no**-bya
to give	dar	dar
to give back	devolver	de-bol-**bair**
glass (for drinking)	el vaso	**ba**-so
(substance)	el cristal	krees**tal**
glasses (spectacles)	las gafas	**ga**-fas
to go	ir	eer
to go back	volver	bol**bair**
to go in	entrar (en)	en**trar** (en)
to go out	salir	sa-**leer**
good	bueno(a)	**bwe**-no(a)
good afternoon	buenas tardes	**bwe**-nas **tar**des
grandchild	el/la nieto(a)	**nye**-to(a)
grandparents	los abuelos	a-**bwe**-los
grapes	las uvas	**oo**bas
great (big)	grande	**gran**de
(wonderful)	estupendo(a)	es-too-**pen**-do(a)
Great Britain	Gran Bretaña	gran bre-**tan**-ya
grey	gris	grees
group	el grupo	**groo**po
guest	el/la invitado(a)	een-bee-**ta**-do(a)
(in hotel)	el/la huésped	**wes**ped
guesthouse	la pensión	pen**syon**
guide (tour guide)	el/la guía	**gee**-a
to guide	guiar	gee-**ar**
guidebook	la guía turística	**gee**-a too-**rees**-tee-ka
guided tour	la visita con guía	bee-**see**-ta kon **gee**-a

H

hair	el pelo	**pe**-lo
hairdresser	el/la peluquero(a)	pe-loo-**ke**-ro(a)
half	medio(a)	**me**-dyo(a)
half an hour	media hora	
half board	media pensión	**me**-dya pen**syon**
half-price	a mitad de precio	a mee-**tad** de **pre**-thyo
ham	el jamón	kha-**mon**
hand	la mano	**ma**-no
handbag	el bolso	**bol**so
hand luggage	el equipaje de mano	e-kee-**pa**-khe de **ma**-no
hand-made	hecho(a) a mano	**e**-cho(a) a **ma**- no
hard	duro(a)	**doo**ro(a)
(difficult)	difícil	dee-**fee**-theel
to have	tener	te-**nair**
to have to	tener que	te-**nair** ke
he	él	el
head	la cabeza	ka-**be**-tha
health	la salud	sa-**lood**
healthy	sano(a)	**sa**-no(a)
to hear	oír	o-**eer**
heart	el corazón	ko-ra-**thon**
heating	la calefacción	ka-le-fak-**thyon**
heavy	pesado(a)	pe-**sa**-do(a)
height	la altura	al-**too**-ra
hello	hola	**o**-la
(on phone)	diga(me)	**dee**ga(me)
to help	ayudar	a-yoo-**dar**
here	aquí	a-**kee**
hi!	¡hola!	¡**o**-la!
high	alto(a)	**al**to(a)
him	él	el
hire (bike, boat, etc)	el alquiler	al-kee-**lair**
to hire	alquilar	al-kee-**lar**
hired car	el coche de alquiler	**ko**-che de al-kee-**lair**
historic	histórico(a)	ees-**to**-ree-ko(a)
to hold	tener	te-**nair**
(to contain)	contener	kon-te-**nair**

hold-up (traffic jam)	el atasco	a-**tas**-ko
holiday	las vacaciones	ba-ka-**thyo**-nes
(public)	la fiesta	**fyes**ta
on holiday	de vacaciones	
home	la casa	**ka**-sa
at home	en casa	
homosexual	homosexual	o-mo-sek-**swal**
hospital	el hospital	os-pee-**tal**
hostel	el hostal	os-**tal**
hot	caliente	ka-**lyen**-te
hour	la hora	**o**-ra
half an hour	media hora	
house	la casa	**ka**-sa
house wine	el vino de la casa	**bee**no de la **ka**-sa
how (in what way)	cómo	**ko**-mo
how much?	¿cuánto?	
how many?	¿cuántos?	
hungry: ***to be hungry***	tener hambre	te-**nair am**bre
hurry:		
I'm in a hurry	tengo prisa	**ten**go **pree**sa

to hurt (injure)	hacer daño	a-**thair da**-nyo
husband	el marido	ma-**ree**-do

I

I	yo	yo
ice	el hielo	**ye**-lo
(cube)	el cubito	koo-**bee**-to
icecream	el helado	e-**la**-do
iced tea	el té helado	te e-**la**-do
identity card	el carné de identidad	kar**ne** de ee-den-tee-**dad**
if	si	see
ill	enfermo(a)	en-**fair**-mo(a)
illness	la enfermedad	en-fair-me-**dad**
immediately	en seguida	en se-**gee**-da
to import	importar	eem-por-**tar**
important	importante	eem-por-**tan**-te
impossible	imposible	eem-po-**see**-ble
to improve	mejorar	me-kho-**rar**
in	dentro de; en	**den**tro de; en

in 10 minutes	dentro de diez minutos	
in London	en Londres	
in front of	delante de	de-**lan**-te de
included	incluido(a)	een-kloo-**ee**-do(a)
indigestion	la indigestión	een-dee-khes-**tyon**
indoors	dentro	**den**tro
infection	la infección	een-fek-**thyon**
information	la información	een-for-ma-**thyon**
ingredients	los ingredientes	een-gre-**dyen**-tes
to injure	herir	e-**reer**
injured	herido(a)	e-**ree**-do(a)
inquiries	información	een-for-ma-**thyon**
insect	el insecto	een-**sek**-to
inside	dentro de	**den**tro de
instant coffee	el café instantáneo	ka-**fe** eens-tan-**ta**-ne-o
instead of	en lugar de	en loo**gar** de
insurance	el seguro	se-**goo**-ro
insurance certificate	la póliza de seguros	**po**-lee-tha de se-**goo**-ros

to insure	asegurar	a-se-goo-**rar**
insured	asegurado(a)	a-se-goo-**ra**-do(a)
interesting	interesante	een-te-re-**san**-te
international	internacional	een-tair-na-thyo-**nal**
into	en	en
into town	al centro	
to introduce to	presentar a	pre-sen-**tar** a
invitation	la invitación	een-bee-ta-**thyon**
to invite	invitar	een-bee-**tar**
Ireland	Irlanda	eer-**lan**-da
Irish	irlandés/irlandesa	eer-lan-**des**/eer-lan-**de**-sa
iron (for clothes)	la plancha	**plan**cha
to iron	planchar	plan**char**
island	la isla	**ees**la
it	lo/la	lo/la
to itch	picar	pee**kar**
it itches	pica	

J

jacket	la chaqueta	cha-**ke**-ta
jam (food)	la mermelada	mair-me-**la**-da
January	enero	e-**ne**-ro
jar (honey, jam, etc)	el tarro	**ta**-rro
jeans	los vaqueros	ba-**ke**-ros
jeweller's	la joyería	kho-ye-**ree**-a
jewellery	las joyas	**kho**yas
job	el empleo	em-**ple**-o
to join (club, etc)	hacerse socio de	a-**thair**-se **so**-thyo de
to join in	participar en	par-tee-thee-**par** en
journey	el viaje	**bya**-khe
juice	el zumo	**thoo**mo
July	julio	**khoo**lyo
to jump	saltar	sal**tar**
June	junio	**khoo**nyo
just: ***just two***	sólo dos	**so**-lo dos

K

to keep (to retain)	guardar	gwar**dar**
key	la llave	**lya**-be
card key (used in hotel)	la llave tarjeta	
to kill	matar	ma-**tar**
kilo(gram)	el kilo(gramo)	**kee**lo, kee-lo-**gra**-mo
kilometre	el kilómetro	kee-**lo**-me-tro
kind (person)	amable	a-**ma**-ble
kind (sort)	la clase	**kla**-se
what kind?	¿qué clase?	
to knock (door)	llamar	lya-**mar**
to know (have knowledge of)	saber	sa-**bair**
(person, place)	conocer	ko-no-**thair**

L

ladies (toilet)	los servicios de señoras	sair-**bee**-thyos de se-**nyo**-ras
lady	la señora	se-**nyo**-ra

lager	la cerveza (rubia)	thair-**be**-tha (**roo**bya)
lamp	la lámpara	**lam**-pa-ra
to land	aterrizar	a-te-rree-**thar**
language	el idioma; la lengua	ee-**dyo**-ma; **len**gwa
large	grande	**gran**de
last	último(a)	**ool**-tee-mo(a)
late	tarde	**tar**de
later	más tarde	mas **tar**de
to laugh	reírse	re-**eer**-se
lavatory (house)	el wáter	**ba**-tair
(in public place)	los servicios	sair-**bee**-thyos
laxative	el laxante	lak-**san**-te
to learn	aprender	a-pren-**dair**
leather	el cuero	**kwe**-ro
to leave (a place)	irse de	**eer**se de
(leave behind)	dejar	de-**khar**
left:		
on/to the left	a la izquierda	a la eeth-**kyair**-da
left-luggage	la consigna	kon-**seeg**-na

leg	la pierna	**pyair**na
lemon	el limón	lee**mon**
lemonade	la gaseosa	ga-se-**o**-sa
length	la longitud	lon-khee-**tood**
lens (photo)	el objetivo	ob-khe-**tee**-bo
(contact lens)	la lentilla	len-**tee**-lya
less	menos	**me**-nos
to let (to allow)	permitir	pair-mee-**teer**
(to hire out)	alquilar	al-kee-**lar**
letter	la carta	**kar**ta
(of alphabet)	la letra	**le**-tra
licence	el permiso	pair-**mee**-so
(driving)	el carné de conducir	kar**ne** de kon-doo-**theer**
to lie down	acostarse	a-kos-**tar**-se
lift (elevator)	el ascensor	as-then-**sor**
light (not heavy)	ligero(a)	lee-**khe**-ro(a)
light	la luz	luth
like (similar to)	como	**ko**-mo
line (row, queue)	la fila	**fee**la
(telephone)	la línea	**lee**-ne-a

list	la lista	**lees**ta
to listen to	escuchar	es-koo-**char**
litre	el litro	**lee**tro
little	pequeño(a)	pe-**ke**-nyo(a)
a little...	un poco de...	
to live	vivir	bee-**beer**
local	de la región; del país	de la re-**khyon**; del pa-**ees**
to lock	cerrar con llave	the-**rrar** kon **lya**-be
long	largo(a)	**lar**go(a)
to look after	cuidar	kwee**dar**
to look at	mirar	mee-**rar**
to look for	buscar	boos**kar**
to lose	perder	pair**dair**
lost	perdido(a)	pair-**dee**-do(a)
lost property office	la oficina de objetos perdidos	o-fee-**thee**-na de ob-**khe**-tos pair-**dee**-dos
lot: ***a lot of***	mucho	**moo**cho
loud (sound, voice)	fuerte	**fwair**te
(volume)	alto(a)	**al**-to(a)

lounge	el salón	sa-**lon**
love	el amor	a-**mor**
to love (person)	querer	ke-**rair**
lovely	precioso(a)	pre-**thyo**-so(a)
low	bajo(a)	**ba**-jo(a)
low-fat	bajo(a) en calorías	**ba**-kho en ka-lo-**ree**-as
lucky: ***to be lucky***	tener suerte	te-**nair swair**te
luggage	el equipaje	e-kee-**pa**-khe
luggage trolley	el carrito	ka-**rree**-to
lunch	la comida	ko-**mee**-da

M

magazine	la revista	re-**bees**-ta
maid (in hotel)	la camarera	ka-ma-**re**-ra
mail	el correo	ko-**rre**-o
by mail	por correo	
main	principal	preen-thee-**pal**
main course (of meal)	el plato principal	**pla**-to preen-thee-**pal**

make-up	el maquillaje	ma-kee-**lya**-khe
male	masculino(a)	mas-koo-**lee**-no
man	el hombre	**om**bre
manager	el/la gerente	khe-**ren**-te
many	muchos(as)	**moo**chos(as)
map (country)	el mapa	**ma**-pa
(of town)	el plano	**pla**-no
March	marzo	**mar**tho
marmalade	la mermelada de naranja	mair-me-**la**-da de na-**ran**-kha
married	casado(a)	ka-**sa**-do(a)
material (cloth)	la tela	**te**-la
to matter	importar	eem-por-**tar**
it doesn't matter	no importa	
May	mayo	**ma**-yo
meal	la comida	ko-**mee**-da
to mean	querer decir	ke-**rair** de-**theer**
to measure	medir	me-**deer**
meat	la carne	**kar**ne
medicine	la medicina	me-dee-**thee**-na

medium rare (meat)	medio(a) hecho(a)	**me**-dyo(a) **e**-cho(a)
to meet (by chance)	encontrarse con	en-kon-**trar**-se kon
(by arrangement)	ver	bair
men	los hombres	**om**bres
menu	la carta	**kar**ta
message	el mensaje	men-**sa**-khe
metre	el metro	**me**-tro
metro (underground)	el metro	**me**-tro
metro station	la estación de metro	es-ta-**thyon** de **me**-tro
middle	el medio	**me**-dyo
midnight	la medianoche	me-dya-**no**-che
at midnight	a medianoche	
milk	la leche	**le**-che
fresh milk	la leche fresca	
hot milk	la leche caliente	
semi-skimmed milk	la leche semidesnatada	

skimmed milk	la leche desnatada	
mineral water	el agua mineral	**a**-gwa mee-ne-**ral**
minimum	el mínimo	**mee**-nee-mo
minute	el minuto	mee-**noo**-to
to miss (train, etc)	perder	pair**dair**
Miss	la señorita	se-nyo-**ree**-ta
missing (lost)	perdido(a)	pair-**dee**-do(a)
my son is missing	se ha perdido mi hijo	
mistake	el error	e-**rror**
mobile (phone)	el teléfono móvil	te-**le**-fo-no **mo**-beel
mobile number	el número de móvil	**noo**-me-ro de **mo**-beel
modern	moderno(a)	mo-**dair**-no(a)
moment	el momento	mo-**men**-to
Monday	el lunes	**loo**nes
money	el dinero	dee-**ne**-ro
month	el mes	mes
more	más	mas
mother	la madre	**ma**-dre
mother-in-law	la suegra	**swe**-gra
motor	el motor	mo-**tor**
motorbike	la moto	**mo**-to
motorway	la autopista	ow-to-**pees**-ta
mouth	la boca	**bo**-ka
to move	mover	mo-**bair**
movie	la película	pe-**lee**-koo-la
Mr	el señor (Sr.)	se-**nyor**
Mrs	la señora (Sra.)	se-**nyo**-ra
Ms	la señora (Sra.)	se-**nyo**-ra
much	mucho(a)	**moo**cho(a)
too much	demasiado(a)	
mugging	el atraco	a-**tra**-ko
muscle	el músculo	**moos**-koo-lo
museum	el museo	mu-**se**-o
music	la música	**moo**-see-ka
must (to have to)	deber	de-**bair**

N

name	el nombre	**nom**bre
napkin	la servilleta	sair-bee-**lye**-ta
narrow	estrecho(a)	es-**tre**-cho(a)
national	nacional	na-thyo-**nal**
nationality	la nacionalidad	na-thyo-na-lee-**dad**
natural	natural	na-too-**ral**
nature	la naturaleza	na-too-ra-**le**-tha
near to	cerca de	**thair**ka de
necessary	necesario(a)	ne-the-**sa**-ryo
to need	necesitar	ne-the-see-**tar**
never	nunca	**noon**ka
new	nuevo(a)	**nwe**-bo(a)
news (TV, radio, etc)	las noticias	no-**tee**-thyas
newspaper	el periódico	pe-**ryo**-dee-ko
New Year	el Año Nuevo	**a**-nyo **nwe**-bo
New Zealand	Nueva Zelanda	**nwe**-ba th-**lan**-da
next	próximo(a)	**prok**-see-mo(a)
nice (person)	simpático(a)	seem-**pa**-tee-ko(a)
(place, holiday)	bonito(a)	bo-**nee**-to(a)
niece	la sobrina	so-**bree**-na
night	la noche	**no**-che
no	no	no
nobody	nadie	**na**-dye
noise	el ruido	**rwee**do
none	ninguno(a)	neen-**goo**-no(a)
non-smoker	el/la no fumador(a)	no foo-ma-**dor**(a)
north	el norte	**nor**te
Northern Ireland	Irlanda del Norte	eer-**lan**-da del **nor**te
nose	la nariz	na-**reeth**
not	no	no
nothing	nada	**na**-da
notice (sign)	el anuncio	a-**noon**-thyo
(warning)	el aviso	a-**bee**-so
November	noviembre	no-**byem**-bre
now	ahora	a-**o**-ra
number	el número	**noo**-me-ro

O

to obtain	obtener	ob-te-**nair**
October	octubre	ok-**too**-bre
of	de	de
off (light, etc)	apagado(a)	a-pa-**ga**-do(a)
(rotten)	pasado(a)	pa-**sa**-do(a)
office	la oficina	o-fee-**thee**-na
often	a menudo	a me-**noo**-do
how often?	¿cada cuánto?	
OK	¡vale!	¡**ba**-le!
old	viejo(a)	**bye**-kho(a)
on (light, TV, machine)	encendido(a)	en-then-**dee**-do(a)
once	una vez	**oo**na beth
at once	en seguida	
only	sólo	**so**-lo
open	abierto(a)	a-**byair**to(a)
to open	abrir	a-**breer**
opposite (to)	enfrente (de)	en-**fren**-te (de)
or	o	o
orange (fruit)	la naranja	na-**ran**-kha
(colour)	naranja	na-**ran**-kha
orange juice	el zumo de naranja	**thoo**mo de na-**ran**-kha
order:		
out of order	averiado(a)	a-be-**rya**-do(a)
to order (in restaurant)	pedir	pe-**deer**
other:		
the other one	el/la otro(a)	**o**-tro(a)
our	nuestro(a)	**nwes**tro(a)
out (light)	apagado(a)	a-pa-**ga**-do(a)
over (on top of)	(por) encima de	(por) en-**thee**-ma de
to be overbooked	tener over-booking	te-**nair** o-bair-**boo**-keen
to overcharge	cobrar de más	ko-**brar** de mas
overdone (food)	demasiado(a) hecho(a)	de-ma-**sya**-do(a) **e**-cho(a)
to owe	deber	de-**bair**
owner	el/la	pro-pye-**ta**-

P

package tour	el viaje organizado	**bya**-khe or-ga-nee-**tha**-do
packet	el paquete	pa-**ke**-te
paid	pagado(a)	pa-**ga**-do(a)
pain	el dolor	do-**lor**
painful	doloroso(a)	do-lo-**ro**-so(a)
painting (picture)	el cuadro	**kwa**-dro
pair	el par	par
palace	el palacio	pa-**la**-thyo
pale	pálido(a)	**pa**-lee-do(a)
pants (men's underwear)	los calzoncillos	kal-thon-**thee**-lyos
paper	el papel	pa-**pel**
parcel	el paquete	pa-**ke**-te
pardon?	¿cómo?	¿**ko**-mo?
parents	los padres	**pa**-dres
park	el parque	**par**ke
to park	aparcar	a-par-**kar**
parking meter	el parquímetro	par-**kee**-me-tro
partner (business)	el/la socio(a)	**so**-thyo(a)
(boy/girlfriend)	el/la compañero(a)	kom-pa-**nye**-ro(a)
party (group)	el grupo	**groo**po
(celebration)	la fiesta	**fyes**ta
passenger	el/la pasajero(a)	pa-sa-**khe**-ro(a)
passport	el pasaporte	pa-sa-**por**-te
pastry (dough)	la masa	**ma**-sa
(cake)	el pastel	pas**tel**
to pay	pagar	pa-**gar**
payment	el pago	**pa**-go
payphone	el teléfono público	te-**le**-fo-no **poo**-blee-ko
peach	el melocotón	me-lo-ko-**ton**
pear	la pera	**pe**-ra
peas	los guisantes	gee-**san**-tes
to peel (fruit)	pelar	pe-**lar**
pen	el bolígrafo; el boli	bo-**lee**-gra-fo; **bo**-lee
pensioner	el/la pensionista	pen-syo-**nees**-ta
people	la gente	**khen**te

pepper (spice)	la pimienta	pee-**myen**-ta
(vegetable)	el pimiento	pee-**myen**-to
per	por	por
per day	al día	
per hour	por hora	
per week	a la semana	
per person	por persona	
perhaps	quizá(s)	kee**tha(s)**
person	la persona	pair-**so**-na
petrol	la gasolina	ga-so-**lee**-na
unleaded petrol	la gasolina sin plomo	
petrol station	la gasolinera	ga-so-lee-**ne**-ra
pharmacy	la farmacia	far-**ma**-thya
phone	el teléfono	te-**le**-fo-no
(mobile)	el móvil	**mo**-beel
by phone	por teléfono	
to phone	llamar por teléfono	lya-**mar** por te-**le**-fo-no
phonebook	la guía (telefónica)	**gee**-a (te-le-**fo**-nee-ka)

phonebox	la cabina (telefónica)	ka-**bee**-na (te-le-**fo**-nee-ka)
phone call	la llamada (telefónica)	lya-**ma**-da (te-le-**fo**-nee-ka)
phonecard	la tarjeta telefónica	tar-**khe**-ta te-le-**fo**-nee-ka
to photocopy	fotocopiar	fo-to-ko-**pyar**
photograph	la fotografía	fo-to-gra-**fee**-a
to take a photograph	hacer una fotografía	
piece	el trozo	**tro**-tho
pillow	la almohada	al-mo-**a**-da
pink	rosa	**ro**-sa
pity: ***what a pity***	¡qué pena!	ike **pe**-na!
place	el lugar	loo**gar**
place of birth	el lugar de nacimiento	loo**gar** de na-thee-**myen**-to
plan (of town)	el plano	**pla**-no
plane (airplane)	el avión	a-**byon**
plaster (sticking)	la tirita®	tee-**ree**-ta
(for broken limb)	la escayola	es-ka-**yo**-la

plastic (made of)	de plástico	de **plas**-tee-ko
platform	el andén	an**den**
play (theatre)	la obra	**o**-bra
to play (games)	jugar	khoo**gar**
pleasant	agradable	a-gra-**da**-ble
please	por favor	por fa-**bor**
pleased	contento(a)	kon-**ten**-to(a)
p.m.	de la tarde	de la **tar**de
pocket	el bolsillo	bol-**see**-lyo
point	el punto	**poon**to
poisonous	venenoso(a)	ve-ne-**no**-so(a)
police (force)	la policía	po-lee-**thee**-a
police station	la comisaría	ko-mee-sa-**ree**-a
pool	la piscina	pees-**thee**-na
poor	pobre	**po**-bre
pork	el cerdo	**thair**do
port (seaport)	el puerto	**pwair**to
(wine)	el oporto	o-**por**-to
porter (hotel)	el portero	por-**te**-ro
(at station)	el mozo	**mo**-tho
possible	posible	po-**see**-ble
post: ***by post***	por correo	por ko-**rre**-o
to post	echar al correo	e-**char** al ko-**rre**-o
postbox	el buzón	boo**thon**
postcard	la postal	pos**tal**
postcode	el código postal	**ko**-dee-go pos**tal**
post office	la oficina de Correos	o-fee-**thee**-na de ko-**rre**-os
potato	la patata	pa-**ta**-ta
pound (weight)	= approx. 0.5 kilo	
(money)	la libra	**lee**bra
to prefer	preferir	pre-fe-**reer**
to prepare	preparar	pre-pa-**rar**
prescription	la receta médica	re-**the**-ta **me**-dee-ka
present (gift)	el regalo	re-**ga**-lo
pretty	bonito(a)	bo-**nee**-to(a)
price	el precio	**pre**-thyo
price list	la lista de precios	**lees**-ta de **pre**-thyos

private	privado(a)	pree-**ba**-do(a)
problem	el problema	pro-**ble**-ma
prohibited	prohibido(a)	pro-ee-**bee**-do(a)
to pronounce	pronunciar	pro-noon-**thyar**
how's it pronounced?	¿cómo se pronuncia?	
to provide	proporcionar	pro-por-thyo-**nar**
public holiday	la fiesta (oficial)	**fyes**ta (o-fee-**thyal**)
pudding	el postre	**pos**tre
to pull	tirar	tee**rar**
purse	el monedero	mo-ne-**de**-ro
to put (place)	poner	po-**nair**
pyjamas	el pijama	pee-**kha**-ma
Pyrenees	los Pirineos	pee-ree-**ne**-os

Q

quality	la calidad	ka-lee-**dad**
quantity	la cantidad	kan-tee-**dad**
question	la pregunta	pre-**goon**-ta
queue	la cola	**ko**-la
to queue	hacer cola	a-**thair ko**-la
quick	rápido(a)	**ra**-pee-do(a)
quickly	de prisa	de **pree**sa
quiet (place)	tranquilo(a)	tran-**kee**-lo(a)
quite	bastante	bas-**tan**-te
quite expensive	bastante caro	

R

race (sport)	la carrera	ka-**rre**-ra
racket (tennis, etc)	la raqueta	ra-**ke**-ta
radio	la radio	**ra**-dyo
railway	el ferrocarril	fe-rro-ka-**rreel**
rain	la lluvia	**lyoo**bya
to rain:		
it's raining	está lloviendo	es**ta** lyo-**byen**-do
raincoat	el impermeable	eem-pair-me-**a**-ble
rape	la violación	byo-la-**thyon**
rare (unique)	excepcional	eks-thep-thyo-**nal**
(steak)	poco hecho(a)	**po**-ko **e**-cho(a)
rate (price)	la tarifa	ta-**ree**-fa

rate of exchange	el tipo de cambio	**tee**po de **kam**byo
raw	crudo(a)	**kroo**do(a)
razor	la maquinilla de afeitar	ma-kee-**nee**-lya de a-fey-**tar**
razor blades	las hojas de afeitar	**o**-khas de a-fey-**tar**
to read	leer	le-**air**
ready	listo(a)	**lees**to(a)
to get ready	prepararse	
real	verdadero(a)	bair-da-**de**-ro(a)
receipt	el recibo	re-**thee**-bo
reception desk	la recepción	re-thep-**thyon**
receptionist	el/la recepcionista	re-thep-thyo-**nees**-ta
to recommend	recomendar	re-ko-men-**dar**
red	rojo(a)	**ro**-kho(a)
to reduce	reducir	re-doo-**theer**
reduction	el descuento	des-**kwen**-to
refund	el reembolso	re-em-**bol**-so
to refuse	negarse	ne-**gar**-se

registered (letter)	certificado(a)	thair-tee-fee-**ka**-do(a)
registration form	la hoja de inscripción	**o**-kha de eens-kreep-**thyon**
to reimburse	reembolsar	re-em-bol-**sar**
relation (family)	el/la pariente	pa-**ryen**-te
relationship	la relación	re-la-**thyon**
to remember	acordarse (de)	a-kor-**dar**-se (de)
I don't remember	no me acuerdo	
to remove	quitar	kee**tar**
repair	la reparación	re-pa-ra-**thyon**
to repair	reparar	re-pa-**rar**
to repeat	repetir	re-pe-**teer**
to reply	contestar	kon-tes-**tar**
to report	informar	een-for-**mar**
reservation	la reserva	re-**sair**-ba
to reserve	reservar	re-sair-**bar**
reserved	reservado(a)	re-sair-**ba**-do(a)
rest (repose)	el descanso	des-**kan**-so
(remainder)	el resto	**res**to

to rest	descansar	des-kan-**sar**
restaurant	el restaurante	res-tow-**ran**-te
restaurant car	el coche restaurante	**ko**-che res-tow-**ran**-te
to return (to go back)	volver	bol**bair**
(to give back)	devolver	de-bol-**bair**
return (ticket)	de ida y vuelta	de **ee**da ee **bwel**ta
rice	el arroz	a-**rroth**
rich (person)	rico(a)	**ree**ko(a)
(food)	pesado(a)	pe-**sa**-do(a)
right (correct)	correcto(a)	ko-**rrek**-to(a)
to be right	tener razón	
right:		
on/to the right	a la derecha	a la de-**re**-cha
to ring (bell, to phone)	llamar	lya-**mar**
ring	el anillo	a-**nee**-lyo
road	la carretera	ka-rre-**te**-ra
road sign	la señal de tráfico	se-**nyal** de **tra**-fee-ko
roadworks	las obras	**o**-bras
roast	asado(a)	a-**sa**-do(a)
roll (bread)	el panecillo	pa-ne-**thee**-lyo
romantic	romántico(a)	ro-**man**-teek-o(a)
room (in house, hotel)	la habitación	a-bee-ta-**thyon**
(space)	sitio	**see**tyo
room number	el número de habitación	**noo**-me-ro de a-bee-ta-**thyon**
room service	el servicio de habitaciones	sair-**bee**-thyo de a-bee-ta-**thyo**-nes
rose	la rosa	**ro**-sa
rosé wine	el (vino) rosado	(**bee**no) ro-**sa**-do
round (shape)	redondo(a)	re-**don**-do(a)
row (line, theatre)	la fila	**fee**la
to run	correr	ko-**rrair**

S

safe (secure) seguro(a) se-**goo**-ro(a)
(for valuables) la caja fuerte **ka**-kha **fwair**te
safety la seguridad se-goo-ree-**dad**
salad la ensalada en-sa-**la**-da
salami el salchichón; el salami sal-chee-**chon**; sa-**la**-mee
sale(s) las rebajas re-**ba**-khas
salesman/woman el/la vendedor(a) ben-de-**dor**(a)
salt la sal sal
same mismo(a) **mees**mo(a)
sand la arena a-**re**-na
sandwich el bocadillo; el sándwich bo-ka-**dee**-lyo; **san**gweech
satellite dish la antena parabólica an-**te**-na pa-ra-**bo**-lee-ka
satellite TV la televisión por satélite te-le-bee-**syon** por sa-**te**-lee-te
Saturday el sábado **sa**-ba-do
sauce la salsa **sal**sa
to save (life) salvar sa**bar**
(money) ahorrar a-o-**rrar**
savoury salado(a) sa-**la**-do(a)
to say decir de-**theer**
scarf (woollen) la bufanda boo-**fan**-da
(headscarf) el pañuelo pa-nyoo-**e**-lo
school la escuela es-**kwe**-la
Scotland Escocia es-**ko**-thya
Scottish escocés/escocesa es-ko-**thes**/es-ko-**the**-sa
sea el mar mar
seafood el/los marisco(s) ma-**rees**-ko(s)
to search buscar boos**kar**
seasick mareado(a) ma-re-**a**-do(a)
seaside la playa **pla**-ya
at the seaside en la playa
season (of year) la estación es-ta-**thyon**
(holiday) la temporada tem-po-**ra**-da
seasonal estacional es-ta-thyo-**nal**
season ticket el abono a-**bo**-no
seasoning el condimento kon-dee-**men**-to

seat (chair)	la silla	**see**lya
(in bus, train)	el asiento	a-**syen**-to
seatbelt	el cinturón de seguridad	theen-too-**ron** de se-goo-ree-**dad**
second	segundo(a)	se-**goon**-do(a)
second (time)	el segundo	se-**goon**-do
second class	de segunda clase	de se-**goon**-da **kla**-se
to see	ver	bair
to sell	vender	ben**dair**
do you sell...?	¿tiene...?	
to send	enviar	en-bee-**ar**
September	septiembre	sep-**tyem**-bre
serious (accident, etc)	grave	**gra**-be
service (in church)	la misa	**mee**-sa
(in restaurant)	el servicio	sair-**bee**-thyo
is service included?	¿está incluido el servicio?	
service charge	el servicio	sair-**bee**-thyo
service station	la estación de servicio	es-ta-**thyon** de sair-**bee**-thyo
serviette	la servilleta	sair-bee-**lye**-ta
set menu	el menú del día	me-**noo** del **dee**-a
several	varios(as)	**ba**-ryos(as)
sex	el sexo	**sek**so
shade	la sombra	**som**bra
shampoo	el champú	cham**poo**
to share	compartir; dividir	kom-par-**teer**; dee-bee-**deer**
to shave	afeitarse	a-fey-**tar**-se
shaver	la maquinilla de afeitar	ma-kee-**nee**-lya de a-fey-**tar**
sheet (bed)	la sábana	**sa**-ba-na
shirt	la camisa	ka-**mee**-sa
shoe	el zapato	tha-**pa**-to
shop	la tienda	**tyen**da
to shop	hacer compras; comprar	a-**thair kom**-pras; kom**prar**

shop assistant	el/la dependiente(a)	de-pen-**dyen**-te(a)
short	corto(a)	**kor**to(a)
shorts	los pantalones cortos	pan-ta-**lo**-nes **kor**tos
shoulder	el hombro	**om**bro
to show	enseñar	en-se-**nyar**
shower (bath)	la ducha	**doo**cha
(rain)	el chubasco	choo-**bas**-ko
shut (closed)	cerrado(a)	the-**rra**-do(a)
sick (ill)	enfermo(a)	en-**fair**-mo(a)
sightseeing:		
to go sightseeing	hacer turismo	a-**thair** too-**rees**-mo
sign	la señal	se-**nyal**
to sign	firmar	feer**mar**
signature	la firma	**feer**ma
silk	la seda	**se**-da
silver	la plata	**pla**-ta
similar to	parecido(a) a	pa-re-**thee**-do(a) a
since (time)	desde	**des**-de
(because)	puesto que	**pwes**to ke
since 1974	desde 1974	
to sing	cantar	kan**tar**
single (unmarried)	soltero(a)	sol-**te**-ro(a)
(bed, room)	individual	een-dee-bee-doo-**al**
sir	señor	se**nyor**
sister	la hermana	air-**ma**-na
to sit	sentarse	sen-**tar**-se
sit down, please	siéntese, por favor	
size (clothes)	la talla	**ta**-lya
(shoes)	el número	**noo**-me-ro
to ski	esquiar	es-kee-**ar**
ski boots	las botas de esquí	**bo**-tas de es**kee**
ski instructor	el/la monitor(a) de esquí	mo-nee-**tor**(a) de es**kee**
skin	la piel	pyel
skirt	la falda	**fal**da

sky	el cielo	**thye**-lo
to sleep	dormir	dor**meer**
sleeping bag	el saco de dormir	**sa**-ko de dor**meer**
slice (of bread)	la rebanada	re-ba-**na**-da
(of ham)	la loncha	**lon**cha
sliced bread	el pan de molde	pan de **mol**de
slow	lento(a)	**len**to(a)
to slow down	reducir la velocidad	re-doo-**theer** la be-lo-thee-**dad**
slowly	despacio	des-**pa**-thyo
small	pequeño(a)	pe-**ke**-nyo(a)
smell	el olor	o-**lor**
smile	la sonrisa	son-**ree**-sa
to smile	sonreir	son-re-**eer**
to smoke	fumar	foo**mar**
smoke	el humo	**oo**mo
snack	el tentempié	ten-ten-**pye**
to have a snack	tomar algo	
to sneeze	estornudar	es-tor-noo-**dar**
snow	la nieve	**nye**-be
to snow	nevar	ne-**bar**
soap	el jabón	kha-**bon**
sober	sobrio(a)	**so**-bryo(a)
sofa	el sofá	so-**fa**
soft	blando	**blan**do
soft drink	el refresco	re-**fres**-ko
some	algunos(as)	al-**goo**-nos(as)
someone	alguien	**al**gyen
something	algo	**al**go
sometimes	a veces	a **be**-thes
son	el hijo	**ee**kho
soon	pronto	**pron**to
as soon as possible	lo antes posible	
sore throat	el dolor de garganta	do-**lor** de gar-**gan**-ta
sorry: ***sorry!***	¡perdón!	¡pair**don**!
soup	la sopa	**so**-pa
south	el sur	soor
souvenir	el souvenir	soo-be-**neer**
Spain	España	es-**pa**-nya
Spanish	español(a)	es-pa-**nyol**(a)

sparkling	espumoso(a)	es-poo-**mo**-so(a)
to speak	hablar	a-**blar**
special	especial	es-pe-**thyal**
speciality	la especialidad	es-pe-thya-lee-**dad**
speed	la velocidad	be-lo-thee-**dad**
speeding	el exceso de velocidad	eks-**the**-so de be-lo-thee-**dad**
speed limit	la velocidad máxima	be-lo-thee-**dad** **mak**-see-ma
spell:		
how is it spelt?	¿cómo se escribe?	¿**ko**-mo se es-**kree**-be?
to spend (money)	gastar	gas**tar**
spicy	picante	pee-**kan**-te
to spill	derramar	de-rra-**mar**
spirits	el alcohol	al**kol**
spoon	la cuchara	koo-**cha**-ra
sport	el deporte	de-**por**-te
sports centre	el polideportivo	po-lee-de-por-**tee**-bo
sports shop	la tienda de deportes	**tyen**da de de-**por**-tes
spring (season)	la primavera	pree-ma-**be**-ra
(metal)	el muelle	**mwe**-lye
square (in town)	la plaza	**pla**-tha
to squeeze	apretar	a-pre-**tar**
(lemon)	exprimir	eks-pree-**meer**
stadium	el estadio	es-**ta**-dyo
stain	la mancha	**man**cha
stairs	las escaleras	es-ka-**le**-ras
stamp (postage)	el sello	**se**-lyo
to stand	estar de pie	es**tar** de pye
star	la estrella	es-**tre**-lya
to start (car)	poner en marcha	po-**nair** en **mar**cha
starter (in meal)	entrante	en-**tran**-te
(in car)	la puesta en marcha	**pwes**ta en **mar**cha
station	la estación	es-ta-**thyon**
stay	la estancia	es-**tan**-thya
to stay (remain)	quedarse	ke-**dar**-se

I'm staying at the hotel...	estoy alojado(a) en el hotel...	
steak	el filete	fee-**le**-te
to steal	robar	ro-**bar**
steel	el acero	a-**the**-ro
steep:		
is it steep?	¿hay mucha subida?	¿aee **moo**cha soo-**bee**-da?
step	el peldaño	pel-**da**-nyo
sterling (pounds)	las libras esterlinas	**lee**bras es-tair-**lee**-nas
to stick (with glue)	pegar	pe-**gar**
still (not fizzy)	sin gas	seen gas
stomach	el estómago	es-**to**-ma-go
stomach upset	el trastorno estomacal	tras-**tor**-no es-to-ma-**kal**
stone	la piedra	**pye**-dra
to stop	parar	pa-**rar**
store (shop)	la tienda	**tyen**da
storm	la tormenta	tor-**men**-ta
(at sea)	el temporal	tem-po-**ral**
story	la historia	ees-**to**-rya
straightaway	inmediatamente	een-me-dya-ta-**men**-te
straight on	todo recto	**to**-do **rek**to
strawberry	la fresa	**fre**-sa
street	la calle	**ka**-lye
street map	el plano de la ciudad	**pla**-no de la thyoo**dad**
strength	la fuerza	**fwair**tha
stroke (medical)	la trombosis	trom-**bo**-sees
strong	fuerte	**fwair**te
student	el/la estudiante	es-too-**dyan**-te
stung	picado(a)	pee-**ka**-do(a)
suddenly	de repente	de re-**pen**-te
suede	el ante	**an**te
sugar	el azúcar	a-**thoo**-kar
sugar-free	sin azúcar	seen a-**thoo**-kar
to suggest	sugerir	soo-khe-**reer**
suit (men's and women's)	el traje	**tra**-khe
suitcase	la maleta	ma-**le**-ta

summer	el verano	be-**ra**-no
sun	el sol	sol
to sunbathe	tomar el sol	to-**mar** el sol
sunblock	la protección solar	pro-tek-**thyon** so-**lar**
sunburn	la quemadura del sol	ke-ma-**doo**-ra del sol
suncream	el protector solar	pro-tek-**tor** so-**lar**
Sunday	el domingo	do-**meen**-go
sunglasses	las gafas de sol	**ga**-fas de sol
sunny:		
it's sunny	hace sol	**a**-the sol
sunscreen	el filtro solar	**feel**tro so-**lar**
sunstroke	la insolación	een-so-la-**thyon**
supermarket	el supermercado	soo-pair-mair-**ka**-do
supper	la cena	**the**-na
supplement	el suplemento	soo-ple-**men**-to
surname	el apellido	a-pe-**lyee**-do
surprise	la sorpresa	sor-**pre**-sa

to survive	sobrevivir	so-bre-bee-**beer**
to sweat	sudar	soo**dar**
sweet (not savoury)	dulce	**dool**the
sweet (dessert)	el dulce	**dool**the
sweetener	el edulcorante	e-dool-ko-**ran**-te
sweets	los caramelos	ka-ra-**me**-los
to swell (injury, etc)	hincharse	een-**char**-se
to swim	nadar	na-**dar**
swimming pool	la piscina	pees-**thee**-na
swimsuit	el bañador	ba-nya-**dor**
to switch off	apagar	a-pa-**gar**
to switch on	encender	en-then-**dair**
swollen	hinchado(a)	een-**cha**-do(a)

T

table	la mesa	**me**-sa
tablet (pill)	la pastilla	pas-**tee**-lya
to take (medicine, etc)	tomar	to-**mar**

how long does it take?	¿cuánto tiempo se tarda?	
to take off	despegar	des-pe-**gar**
to take out (of bag, etc)	sacar	sa-**kar**
to talk to	hablar con	a-**blar** kon
tall	alto(a)	**al**to(a)
taste	el sabor	sa-**bor**
to taste	probar	pro-**bar**
can I taste it?	¿puedo probarlo?	
tax	el impuesto	eem-**pwes**-to
taxi	el taxi	**tak**see
tea	el té	te
teeth	los dientes	**dyen**tes
telephone	el teléfono	te-**le**-fo-no
to telephone	llamar por teléfono	lya-**mar** por te-**le**-fo-no
telephone box	la cabina (telefónica)	ka-**bee**-na (te-le-**fo**-nee-ka)
telephone call	la llamada (telefónica)	lya-**ma**-da (te-le-**fo**-nee-ka)
telephone card	la tarjeta telefónica	tar-**khe**-ta te-le-**fo**-nee-ka
telephone directory	la guía (telefónica)	la guía (te-le-**fo**-nee-ka)
telephone number	el número de teléfono	**noo**-me-ro de te-**le**-fo-no
television	la televisión	te-le-bee-**syon**
to tell	decir	de-**theer**
temperature	la temperatura	tem-pe-ra-**too**-ra
to have a temperature	tener fiebre	te-**nair fye**-bre
temporary	provisional	pro-bee-syo-**nal**
tennis	el tenis	**te**-nees
to test (try out)	probar	pro-**bar**
to thank	agradecer	a-gra-de-**thair**
thank you	gracias	**gra**-thyas
that	ese/esa	**e**-se/**e**-sa
that one	ése/ésa/eso	
the	el/la/los/las	el/la/los/las
theatre	el teatro	te-**a**-tro
theft	el robo	**ro**-bo

there (over there)	allí	a-**lyee**
there is/ there are	hay	aee
these	estos/estas	**es**tos/**es**tas
they	ellos/ellas	**e**-lyos/**e**-lyas
thick (not thin)	grueso(a)	**grwe**-so(a)
thief	el ladrón/ la ladrona	la-**dron**/ la-**dro**-na
thin (person)	delgado(a)	del-**ga**-do(a)
thing	la cosa	**ko**-sa
my things	mis cosas	
to think	pensar	pen**sar**
thirsty: *I'm thirsty*	tengo sed	**ten**go sed
this	este/esta/esto	**es**te/**es**ta/**es**to
this one	éste/ésta	
those	esos/esas	**e**-sos/**e**-sas
those ones	ésos/ésas	
throat	la garganta	gar-**gan**-ta
thunderstorm	la tormenta	tor-**men**-ta
Thursday	el jueves	**khwe**-bes
ticket (bus, etc)	el billete	bee-**lye**-te
ticket office	el despacho de billetes	des-**pa**-cho de bee-**lye**-tes
tidy	arreglado(a)	a-rre-**gla**-do(a)
to tidy up	ordenar	or-de-**nar**
tie	la corbata	kor-**ba**-ta
tight (fitting)	ajustado(a)	a-khoos-**ta**-do(a)
tights	las medias	**me**-dyas
till (cash desk)	la caja	**ka**-kha
(until)	hasta	**as**-ta
till 2 o'clock	hasta las 2	
time	el tiempo	**tyem**po
(clock)	la hora	**o**-ra
timetable	el horario	o-**ra**-ryo
tip	la propina	pro-**pee**-na
tired	cansado(a)	kan-**sa**-do(a)
tissues	los kleenex®	**klee**neks
to	a	a
to the airport	al aeropuerto	
toast (to eat)	la tostada	tos-**ta**-da
(raising glass)	el brindis	**breen**dees
tobacco	el tabaco	ta-**ba**-ko

tobacconist's	el estanco	el es-**tan**-ko
today	hoy	oy
together	juntos(as)	**khoon**tos(as)
toilet	los aseos; los servicios	a-**se**-os; sair-**bee**-thyos
toilet for disabled	los servicios para minusválidos	
tomato	el tomate	to-**ma**-te
tomorrow	mañana	ma-**nya**-na
tongue	la lengua	**len**gwa
tonic water	la tónica	**to**-nee-ka
tonight	esta noche	**es**ta **no**-che
too (also)	también	tam**byen**
tooth	el diente	**dyen**te
toothache	el dolor de muelas	do-**lor** de **mwe**-las
toothbrush	el cepillo de dientes	the-**pee**-lyo de **dyen**tes
toothpaste	la pasta de dientes	**pas**ta de **dyen**tes
top (of hill)	la cima	**thee**ma
(shirt)	el top	top
(t-shirt)	la camiseta	ka-mee-**se**-ta
on top of...	sobre...	
total (amount)	el total	to-**tal**
tour (trip)	el viaje	**bya**-khe
(of museum, etc)	la visita	bee-**see**-ta
guided tour	la visita con guía	
tourist	el/la turista	too-**rees**-ta
tourist office	la oficina de turismo	o-fee-**thee**-na de too-**rees**-mo
town	la ciudad	thyoo**dad**
town centre	el centro de la ciudad	**then**tro de la thyoo**dad**
town hall	el ayuntamiento	a-yoon-ta-**myen**-to
town plan	el plano de la ciudad	**pla**-no de la thyoo**dad**
toy	el juguete	khoo-**ge**-te
traditional	tradicional	tra-dee-thyo-**nal**

traffic jam	el atasco	a-**tas**-ko
traffic lights	el semáforo	se-**ma**-fo-ro
traffic warden	el/la guardia de tráfico	**gwar**dya de **tra**-fee-ko
trailer	el remolque	re-**mol**-ke
train	el tren	tren
by train	en tren	
tram	el tranvía	tran-**bee**-a
to translate	traducir	tra-doo-**theer**
to travel	viajar	bya-**khar**
travel agent's	la agencia de viajes	a-**khen**-thya de **bya**-khes
trip	la excursión	eks-koor-**syon**
trolley	el carrito	ka-**rree**-to
trouble	el apuro	a-**poo**-ro
to be in trouble	estar en apuros	
trousers	los pantalones	pan-ta-**lo**-nes
true	verdadero(a)	bair-da-**de**-ro(a)
to try (attempt)	probar	pro-**bar**
to try on (clothes)	probarse	pro-**bar**-se
t-shirt	la camiseta	ka-mee-**se**-ta
Tuesday	el martes	**mar**tes
to turn	girar	gee**rar**
to turn around	girar	gee**rar**
to turn off (light, etc)	apagar	a-pa-**gar**
(tap)	cerrar	the-**rrar**
to turn on (light, etc)	encender	en-then-**dair**
(tap)	abrir	a-**breer**
twice	dos veces	dos **be**-thes
typical	típico(a)	**tee**-pee-ko(a)

U

ugly	feo(a)	**fe**-o(a)
umbrella	el paraguas	pa-**ra**-gwas
(sunshade)	la sombrilla	som-**bree**-lya
uncle	el tío	**tee**-o
uncomfortable	incómodo(a)	een-**ko**-mo-do(a)
under	debajo de	de-**ba**-kho de
underground	el metro	**me**-tro
to understand	entender	en-ten-**dair**

I don't understand	no entiendo	
do you understand?	¿entiende?	
underwear	la ropa interior	**ro**-pa een-te-**ryor**
United Kingdom	el Reino Unido	**rey**no oo-**nee**-do
United States	Estados Unidos	es-**ta**-dos oo-**nee**-dos
unleaded petrol	la gasolina sin plomo	ga-so-**lee**-na seen **plo**-mo
to unpack (suitcases)	deshacer las maletas	de-sa-**thair** las ma-**le**-tas
up: ***to get up***	levantarse	le-ban-**tar**-se
urgent	urgente	oor-**khen**-te
to use	usar	oo**sar**
useful	útil	**oo**teel

V

vacancy (in hotel)	la habitación libre	a-bee-ta-**thyon lee**bre
vacant	libre	**lee**bre
valid	válido(a)	**ba**-lee-do(a)
valley	el valle	**ba**-lye
valuable	de valor	de ba-**lor**
valuables	los objetos de valor	ob-**khe**-tos de ba-**lor**
value	el valor	ba-**lor**
VAT	el IVA	**ee**ba
vegetables	las verduras	bair-**doo**-ras
vegetarian	vegetariano(a)	be-khe-ta-**rya**-no(a)
very	muy	mwee
vest	la camiseta	ka-mee-**se**-ta
vet	el/la veterinario(a)	be-te-ree-**na**-ryo (a)
via	por	por
view	la vista	**bees**ta
village	el pueblo	**pwe**-blo
vinegar	el vinagre	bee-**na**-gre
virus	el virus	**bee**roos
visa	el visado	bee-**sa**-do

visit	la visita	bee-**see**-ta
to visit	visitar	bee-see-**tar**
visitor	el/la visitante	bee-see-**tan**-te
voice	la voz	both
to vomit	vomitar	bo-mee-**tar**
voucher	el vale; el bono	**ba**-le; **bo**-no

W

to wait for	esperar	es-pe-**rar**
waiter/waitress	el/la camarero(a)	ka-ma-**re**-ro(a)
waiting room	la sala de espera	**sa**-la de es-**pe**-ra
Wales	Gales	**ga**-les
walk	un paseo	oon pa-**se**-o
to go for a walk	dar un paseo	
to walk	andar	an**dar**
wallet	la cartera	kar-**te**-ra
to want	querer	ke-**rair**
I want	quiero	
warm	caliente	ka-**lyen**-te
it's warm (weather)	hace calor	
to warm up (milk, etc)	calentar	ka-len-**tar**
to wash (oneself)	lavar(se)	la-**bar**(se)
to watch (look at)	mirar	mee**rar**
watch	el reloj	re-**lokh**
water	el agua	**a**-gwa
drinking water	el agua potable	
hot/cold water	el agua caliente/fría	
watermelon	la sandía	san-**dee**-a
way (manner)	la manera	ma-**ne**-ra
(route)	el camino	ka-**mee**-no
way in (entrance)	la entrada	en-**tra**-da
way out (exit)	la salida	sa-**lee**-da
weak (coffee, tea)	poco cargado(a)	**po**-ko kar-**ga**-do(a)
to wear	llevar	lye-**bar**
weather	el tiempo	**tyem**po
wedding	la boda	**bo**-da
Wednesday	el miércoles	**myair**-ko-les
week	la semana	se-**ma**-na

last week	la semana pasada	
next week	la semana que viene	
per week	por semana	
this week	esta semana	
weekend	el fin de semana	feen de se-**ma**-na
weekly	semanal	se-ma-**nal**
weight	el peso	**pe**-so
welcome!	¡bienvenido(a)!	¡byen-be-**nee**-do(a)!
well done (steak)	muy hecho(a)	mwee **e**-cho(a)
Welsh	galés/galesa	ga-**les**/ga-**les**-a
(language)	el galés	ga-**les**
west	el oeste	o-**es**-te
wet	mojado(a)	mo-**kha**-do(a)
(weather)	lluvioso(a)	lyoo-**byo**-so(a)
what?	¿qué?	¿ke?
when?	¿cuándo?	¿**kwan**do?
where?	¿dónde?	¿**don**de?
which?	¿cuál?	¿kwal?
which one?	¿cuál?	
which ones?	¿cuáles?	

while: ***in a while***	dentro de un rato	**den**tro de oon **ra**-to
white	blanco(a)	**blan**ko(a)
who?	¿quién?	¿kyen?
whole	entero(a)	en-**te**-ro(a)
wholemeal bread	el pan integral	pan een-te-**gral**
whose?	¿de quién?	¿de kyen?
why?	¿por qué?	¿por ke?
wide	ancho(a)	**an**cho(a)
wife	la mujer	moo**khair**
to win	ganar	ga-**nar**
wind	el viento	**byen**to
window	la ventana	ben-**ta**-na
(shop)	el escaparate	es-ka-pa-**ra**-te
(in car, train)	la ventanilla	ben-ta-**nee**-lya
wine	el vino	**bee**no
wine list	la carta de vinos	**kar**ta de **bee**nos
winter	el invierno	een-**byair**-no
with	con	kon
with ice	con hielo	

with milk	con leche	
with sugar	con azúcar	
without	sin	seen
without ice	sin hielo	
without milk	sin leche	
without sugar	sin azúcar	
woman	la mujer	moo**khair**
word	la palabra	pa-**la**-bra
work	el trabajo	tra-**ba**-kho
to work (person)	trabajar	tra-ba-**khar**
(machine, car)	funcionar	foon-thyo-**nar**
world	el mundo	**moon**do
worried	preocupado(a)	pre-okoo-**pa**-do(a)
worse	peor	pe-**or**
to write	escribir	es-kree-**beer**
please write it down	escríbalo, por favor	
wrong:		
what's wrong	¿qué pasa?	¿ke **pa**-sa?

X

X-ray	la radiografía	ra-dyo-gra-**fee**-a
to x-ray	hacer una radiografía	a-**thair oo**na ra-dyo-gra-**fee**-a

Y

year	el año	**a**nyo
this year	este año	
next year	el año que viene	
last year	el año pasado	
yellow	amarillo(a)	a-ma-**ree**-lyo(a)
Yellow Pages	las páginas amarillas	**pa**-khee-nas a-ma-**ree**-lyas
yes	sí	see
yesterday	ayer	a-**yair**
yoghurt	el yogur	yo-**goor**
young	joven	**kho**-ben

Z

zone	la zona	**tho**-na
zoo	el zoo	**tho**-o

Spanish – English

A

a to; at
a la estación to the station
a las 4 at 4 o'clock
abajo below; downstairs
abierto(a) open
abrigo *m* coat
abril *m* April
abrir to open; to turn on *(tap)*
abuela *f* grandmother
abuelo *m* grandfather
acabar to finish
acampar to camp
acceso *m* access
acceso prohibido no access
acceso vías to the platforms
accidente *m* accident
aceite *m* oil
aceite de oliva olive oil
aceituna *f* olive
aceptar to accept
acompañar to accompany
acuerdo *m* agreement
¡de acuerdo! OK; alright
alojamiento y desayuno bed and breakfast
adelante forward
adiós goodbye; bye
admitir to accept; to permit
no se admiten... ...not permitted
aduana *f* customs
adulto(a) *m/f* adult
aerolínea *f* airline
aeropuerto *m* airport
afeitarse to shave
aficionado(a) *m/f* fan *(cinema, jazz, etc)*
agencia *f* agency
agencia inmobiliaria estate agent's
agenda *f* diary; personal organizer
agente de policía policeman/woman
agosto *m* August
agradecer to thank
agua *f* water
agua caliente/fría hot/cold water
agua mineral mineral water
ahora now
ahorrar to save *(money)*
ahumado(a) smoked
aire *m* air
aire acondicionado air-conditioning
alarma *f* alarm
albaricoque *m* apricot
albergue *m* hostel

alcanzar to reach; to get
alcohol *m* alcohol; spirits
alcohólico(a) alcoholic
alergia *f* allergy
alérgico(a) a allergic to
algo something
algodón *m* cotton
alguien someone
alguno(a) some; any
algunos(as) some; a few
alimentación *f* grocer's; food
alimento *m* food
allí there *(over there)*
almacén *m* store; warehouse
grandes almacenes department stores
almendra *f* almond
almohada *f* pillow
almuerzo *m* lunch
alojamiento *m* accommodation
alquilar to rent; to hire
se alquila for hire
alquiler *m* rent; rental
alquiler de coches car hire
alrededor about; around
alto(a) high; tall
alta tensión high voltage
altura *f* altitude; height
amable pleasant; kind
amarillo(a) yellow; amber *(traffic light)*
ambulancia *f* ambulance
ambulatorio *m* health centre
América del Norte *f* North America
amigo(a) *mf* friend
amor *m* love
analgésico *m* painkiller
análisis *m* analysis
ancho *m* width
anchoa *f* anchovy *(salted)*
Andalucía *f* Andalusia
andaluz(a) Andalusian
andar to walk
andén *m* platform
angina (de pecho) *f* angina
anillo *m* ring
animal *m* animal
aniversario *m* anniversary
año *m* year
Año Nuevo New Year
ante *m* suede
antes (de) before
anticonceptivo *m* contraceptive
antigüedades *tfpl* antiques
antiguo(a) old; ancient
antihistamínico *m* antihistamine

Spanish - English

anular	to cancel
anunciar	to announce; to advertise
anuncio *m*	advertisement; notice
apagado(a)	off *(light, etc)*
apagar	to switch off; to turn off
aparato *m*	appliance
aparato de aire acondicionado	air-conditioning unit
aparcamiento *m*	car park
aparcar	to park
apartamento *m*	flat; apartment
apellido *m*	surname
apendicitis *f*	appendicitis
aperitivo *m*	aperitif *(drink)*; appetizer; snack *(food)*
aprender	to learn
aquí	here
árbol *m*	tree
ardor de estómago *m*	heartburn
arena *f*	sand
armario *m*	wardrobe; cupboard
arreglar	to fix; to mend
arriba	upstairs; above
hacia arriba	upward(s)
arroz *m*	rice
arte *m*	art
artesanía *f*	crafts
articulación *f*	joint *(body)*
artículo *m*	article
artículos de regalo	gifts
asado(a)	roast
ascensor *m*	lift
asegurado(a)	insured
asegurar	to insure
aseos *mpl*	toilets
asiento *m*	seat
asistencia *f*	help; assistance
asistencia técnica	repairs
atacar	to attack
ataque *m*	fit *(seizure)*
ataque al corazón	heart attack
ataque de asma	asthma attack
atención *f*	attention
atención al cliente	customer service
aterrizar	to land
atraco *m*	mugging *(person)*
atrás	behind
atropellar	to knock down *(car)*
atún *m*	tuna fish
auténtico(a)	genuine; real
autobús *m*	bus

autocar *m* — coach (bus)
autopista *f* — motorway
autor(a) *mf* — author
autoservicio *m* — self-service
Av./Avda. — *abbrev. for* **avenida**
avena *f* — oats
avenida *f* — avenue
avería *f* — breakdown *(car)*
averiado(a) — out of order; broken down
avión *m* — airplane
aviso *m* — notice; warning
ayer — yesterday
ayudar — to help
ayuntamiento *m* — town/city hall
azafata *f* — air hostess; stewardess
azúcar *m* — sugar
azul — blue

bahía *f* — bay *(along coast)*
bailar — to dance
baile *m* — dance
bajar — to go down(stairs); to drop *(temperature)*
bajarse (del) — to get off *(bus, etc)*
bajo(a) — low; short; soft *(sound)*
balcón *m* — balcony
balón *m* — ball
bañador *m* — swimming costume/trunks
bañarse — to go swimming; to bathe; to have a bath
baño *m* — bath; bathroom
con baño — with bath

barato(a) — cheap
barbacoa *f* — barbecue
barco *m* — ship; boat
barrio *m* — district; suburb
bastante — enough; quite
batido *m* — milkshake
to be — ser; estar
bebé *m* — baby
beber — to drink
bebida *f* — drink
bebida sin alcohol — soft drink
berenjena *f* — aubergine/eggplant
besar — to kiss
beso *m* — kiss
biberón *m* — baby's bottle
bicicleta *f* — bicycle
bicicleta de montaña — mountain bike

Spanish – English

bien	well, good
bienvenido(a)	welcome
billete *m*	ticket
billete de ida	single ticket
billete de ida y vuelta	return ticket
bistec *m*	steak
blanco(a)	white
blando(a)	soft
blusa *f*	blouse
boca *f*	mouth
bocadillo *m*	sandwich *(made with French bread)*
boda *f*	wedding
bolígrafo *m*	biro; pen
bollo *m*	roll; bun
bolsa *f*	bag; Stock Exchange
bolsa de plástico	plastic bag
bomberos *mpl*	fire brigade
bombilla *f*	light bulb
bombones *mpl*	chocolates
bonito(a)	pretty; nice-looking
bono *m*	voucher
bonobús *m*	bus pass
borracho(a)	drunk
bosque *m*	forest; wood
bota *f*	boot
bote *m*	boat; tin; can
bote salvavidas	lifeboat
botella *f*	bottle
botón *m*	button
bragas *fpl*	knickers
brazo *m*	arm
brillar	to shine
británico(a)	British
bronceado(a)	sun-tanned
bronceador *m*	suntan lotion
bueno(a)	good; fine
¡buenos días!	good morning!
¡buenas tardes!	good afternoon/ evening!
¡buenas noches!	good evening/ night!
bufanda *f*	scarf *(woollen)*
buscar	to look for
butacas *fpl*	stalls *(theatre)*
buzón *m*	postbox; letterbox
buzón de voz	voicemail

C

caballeros *mpl*	gents
caballo *m*	horse
montar a caballo	to go riding
cabello *m*	hair
cabeza *f*	head

cabina ***(telefónica)***	phone box
cable *m*	wire; cable
cacahuete *m*	peanut
cacao *m*	cocoa
cada	every; each
cada día	daily *(each day)*
cada uno	each (one)
cadena	chain; channel *(TV)*; WC chain *(for cistern)*
caducado(a)	out-of-date
café *m*	café; coffee
cafetería *f*	snack bar; café
caja *f*	cashdesk; box
caja de cambios	gearbox
caja fuerte	safe
cajero automático	cash dispenser; ATM
calamares *mpl*	squid
calambre *m*	cramp
caldo *m*	stock; consommé
calefacción *f*	heating
calentar	to heat up *(milk, etc)*
calidad *f*	quality
caliente	hot
calle *f*	street; fairway *(golf)*
calmante *m*	painkiller
calzado *m*	footwear
calzoncillos *mpl*	underpants
cama *f*	bed
camarera *f*	waitress; chambermaid
camarero *m*	barman; waiter
cambiar	to change; to exchange
cambiarse	to get changed
cambio *m*	change; exchange; gear *(car)*
caminar	to walk
camino *m*	path; road; route
camión *m*	lorry
camisa *f*	shirt
camiseta *f*	t-shirt; vest
camisón *m*	nightdress
camping *m*	campsite
campo *m*	countryside; field; pitch
campo de fútbol	football pitch
campo de golf	golf course
caña *f*	cane; rod
caña (de cerveza)	glass of beer
caña de pescar	fishing rod
Canadá *m*	Canada
canadiense	Canadian
cancelación *f*	cancellation

cancelar	to cancel
cansado(a)	tired
cantidad *f*	quantity
capilla *f*	chapel
cara *f*	face
caramelo *m*	sweet; caramel
caravana *f*	caravan
carburante *m*	fuel
carga *m*	charge
cargador *m*	recharger
cargar	to load; charge
cargar en cuenta	to charge to account
cargo *m*	charge
a cargo del cliente	at the customer's expense
carne *f*	meat
carné de conducir *m*	driving licence
carné de identidad (DNI) *m*	identity card
carnicería *f*	butcher's
caro(a)	dear; expensive
carretera *f*	road
carretera comarcal	secondary road, B-road
carretera nacional	A-road
carretera de circunvalación	ring road
carril *m*	lane *(on road)*
carta *f*	letter; playing card; menu
carta certificada	registered letter
cartera *f*	wallet; briefcase
casa *f*	house; home; household
casado(a)	married
casi	almost
caso: ***en caso de***	in case of
castañuelas *fpl*	castanets
castellano(a)	Spanish; Castilian
castillo *m*	castle
católico(a)	Catholic
cava *m*	cava; sparkling white wine
ceder	to give way
ceda el paso	give way
celo *m*	Sellotape®
cementerio *m*	cemetery
cena *f*	dinner; supper
cenar	to have dinner
cenicero *m*	ashtray
centímetro *m*	centimetre
céntimo *m*	euro cent
centro *m*	centre
centro de	business centre

cepillo *m* brush
cepillo de dientes toothbrush
cerámica *f* ceramics; pottery
cerca (de) near; close to
cercanías *fpl* outskirts
tren de cercanías suburban train
cerdo *m* pig; pork
cereza *f* cherry
cerillas *fpl* matches
cerrado(a) closed
cerrado por reforma closed for repairs
cerradura *f* lock
certificado *m* certificate
certificado(a) registered
cervecería *f* pub
cerveza *f* beer; lager

chalet *(sing)*, **chalets** *(pl)* *m* villa
chaleco *m* waistcoat
chaleco salvavidas life jacket
champiñón *m* mushroom
champú *m* shampoo
chaqueta *f* jacket
charcutería *f* delicatessen
cheque *m* cheque
cheque de viaje traveller's cheque
chica *f* girl
chico *m* boy
chico(a) small
chocar to crash *(car)*
chocolate *m* chocolate; hot chocolate
chorizo *m* hard pork sausage
chuleta *f* cutlet; chop

ciclista *mf* cyclist
ciego(a) blind
cigarrillo *m* cigarette
cigarro *m* cigar; cigarette
cine *m* cinema
cinturón *m* belt
cinturón de seguridad safety belt
circulación *f* traffic
circule por la derecha keep right *(road sign)*
cita *f* appointment
ciudad *f* city; town
claro(a) light *(colour)*; clear
clase *f* class; type; lesson
clase preferente club/business class
clase turista economy class
cliente *mf* customer; client

Spanish – English

climatizado(a) air-conditioned
clínica *f* clinic; private hospital
cobrar to charge; to cash
coche *m* car; coach *(on train)*
cocina *f* kitchen; cooker; cuisine
cocinar to cook
coco *m* coconut
codo *m* elbow
coger to catch; to get; to pick up *(phone)*
cola *f* glue; queue; tail
colchón *m* mattress
colegio *m* school
colisionar to crash
collar *m* necklace
color *m* colour
comenzar to begin
comer to eat
comestibles *mpl* groceries
comida *f* food; meal
se sirven comidas meals served
comidas caseras home cooking
comisaría *f* police station
como as; like; since
¿cómo? how?; pardon?
cómodo(a) comfortable
completo(a) full; no vacancies
compras shopping
comprar to buy
comprender to understand
con with
condón *m* condom
conducir to drive
conductor(a) *mf* driver
confirmación *f* confirmation
confirmar to confirm
congelado(a) frozen
congelador *m* freezer
conocer to know; to be acquainted with
consumir to eat; to use
consumir (preferentemente) antes de... best before...
contacto *m* contact; ignition *(car)*
contagioso(a) infectious
contaminado(a) polluted
contento(a) pleased
contestar to answer; to reply
contra against
contrato *m* contract
control *m* inspection; check

control de seguridad security check
copa *f* glass; goblet
copa de helado mixed ice cream
cordero *m* lamb; mutton
correcto(a) right *(correct)*
correo *m* mail
correo electrónico e-mail
Correos *m* post office
correr to run
corrida de toros *f* bullfight
corriente *f* power; current *(electric, water)*; draught *(of air)*
cortado *m* espresso coffee with dash of milk
cortar to cut
corte *m* cut

corto(a) short
cosa *f* thing
costa *f* coast
costar to cost
crédito *m* credit
creer to think; to believe
crema *f* cream *(lotion)*
crema bronceadora/solar suntan lotion
crema de afeitar shaving cream
cruce *m* junction; crossroads
crudo(a) raw
cruzar to cross
cuadro *m* picture; painting
a/de cuadros checked *(pattern)*
¿cuál? which?
¿cuándo? when?
¿cuánto? how much?
¿cuántos? how many?

cuarto *m* room
cuarto de baño bathroom
cuarto de estar living room
cubrir to cover
cuchara *f* spoon
cucharilla *f* teaspoon
cuchillo *m* knife
cuenta *f* bill; account
cuero *m* leather
cuidado *m* care
¡cuidado! look out!
¡ten cuidado! be careful!
cumpleaños *m* birthday
curvas peligrosas *fpl* dangerous bends

D

dar to give
dar marcha atrás to reverse
dar propina to tip *(waiter, etc)*

Spanish - English

datos *mpl*	data; information
dcha.	*abbrev. for* **derecha**
de	of; from
de acuerdo	all right *(agreed)*
debajo (de)	under(neath)
deber	to owe; to have to
decir	to tell; to say
declarar	to declare
dedo *m*	finger
dejar	to let; to leave
dejar libre la salida	keep clear
delante de	in front of
delito *m*	crime
demasiado	too much
demasiado hecho(a)	overdone
dentro (de)	inside
dependiente(a) *mf*	sales assistant
deporte *m*	sport
depósito de gasolina *m*	petrol tank
derecha *f*	right(-hand side)
a la derecha *mf*	on/to the right
derecho *m*	right; law
derechos de aduana	customs duty
derecho(a)	right; straight
desayuno *m*	breakfast
descafeinado(a)	decaffeinated
descansar	to rest
descanso *m*	rest; interval
descongelar	to defrost; to de-ice
descuento *m*	discount; reduction
desde	since; from
desenchufado(a)	off; disconnected; unplugged
deshacer	to undo; to unpack
desinfectante *m*	disinfectant
desmaquilladora	make-up remover
desnatado(a)	skimmed
desodorante *m*	deodorant
despacio	slowly; quietly
despegar	to take-off; to remove; to peel off
despertador *m*	alarm (clock)
después	after; afterward(s)
destino *m*	destination
desvío *m*	detour; diversion

detalle *m*	detail; nice gesture
al detalle	retail
detener	to arrest
detrás (de)	behind
día *m*	day
día festivo/ de fiesta	public holiday; holiday
día laborable/ hábil	working day; weekday
diabético(a) *mf*	diabetic
diario(a)	daily
a diario	every day
diarrea *f*	diarrhoea
diciembre *m*	December
diente *m*	tooth
dieta *f*	diet
difícil	difficult
dificultad *f*	difficulty
dinero *m*	money
dinero (en) efectivo	cash
dirección *f*	direction; address; *(Aut)* steering; steering wheel
dirección de correo electrónico	e-mail address
dirección prohibida	no entry
dirección única	one-way
directo(a)	direct *(train, etc)*
disponible	available
distancia *f*	distance
distinto(a)	different
diversión *f*	fun
divertido(a)	funny *(amusing)*
divertirse	to enjoy oneself
divisa *f*	foreign currency
divorciado(a)	divorced
docena *f*	dozen
documentos *mpl*	documents
dolor *m*	ache; pain
dolor de cabeza	headache
dolor de garganta	sore throat
dolor de muelas	toothache
dolor de oídos	earache
domicilio *m*	home address
domingo *m*	Sunday
¿dónde?	where?
dormir	to sleep
dormitorio *m*	bedroom
dosis *f*	dose; dosage
droga *f*	drug
ducha *f*	shower
ducharse	to take a shower
dueño(a) *mf*	owner
durante	during

Spanish – English

E

ecológico(a) organic; environmentally friendly
edad *f* age *(of person)*
edad mínima age limit
EE.UU. USA
el the
él he; him
electricidad *f* electricity
electricista *mf* electrician
elegir to choose
ella she; her
ello it
ellos(as) they; them
embajada *f* embassy
embarazada pregnant
embarque *m* boarding
empezar to begin
empleo *m* employment;
empresa *f* firm; company
empujar to push
empuje push
en in; into; on
encender to switch on; to light
encender las luces switch on headlights
enchufe *m* plug; point; socket
encima de onto; on top of
encontrar to find
encontrarse con to meet *(by chance)*
enero *m* January
enfadado(a) angry
enfermedad *f* disease
enfermera(o) *mf* nurse
enfermo(a) ill
enfrente (de) opposite
ensalada *f* salad
enseñar to show; to teach
entender to understand
entero(a) whole
entrada *f* entrance; admission; ticket
entrada principal main entrance
entradas limitadas limited tickets
entradas numeradas numbered tickets
no hay entradas sold out
entrada libre admission free
entrar to go in; to get in; to enter
entre among; between

enviar to send
envío *m* shipment
envolver to wrap
epiléptico(a) epileptic
equipaje *m* luggage; baggage
equipaje de mano hand-luggage
error *m* mistake
es he/she/it is
escalera *f* stairs; ladder
escalera de incendios fire escape
escaparate *m* shop window
escoba *f* broom *(brush)*
escocés(cesa) Scottish
Escocia *f* Scotland
escoger to choose
esconder to hide
escribir to write
escrito: ***por escrito*** in writing
escuchar to listen to
escultura *f* sculpture
ese/esa that
esos/esas those
espacio *m* space
espalda *f* back *(of body)*
España *f* Spain
español(a) Spanish
especialidad *f* speciality
espectáculo *m* entertainment; show
espejo *m* mirror
espejo retrovisor rear-view mirror
esperar to wait (for); to hope
esposa *f* wife
esposo *m* husband
esquí *m* skiing; ski
esquí acuático water-skiing
esquí de fondo cross-country skiing
esquiar to ski
esquina *f* street corner
está you *(formal)*/ he/she/it is
estación *f* railway station; season
estación de autobuses bus/coach station
estación de servicio petrol/service station
estadio *m* stadium
Estados Unidos *mpl* United States
estanco *m* tobacconist's
estar to be
este *m* east
éste/esta this
estómago *m* stomach

Spanish – English

estos/éstas these
estrecho(a) narrow
estrella *f* star
estropeado(a) out of order; broken; damaged
euro *m* euro
Europa *f* Europe
evitar to avoid
excursión *f* tour; excursion
éxito *m* success
explicar to explain
exportar to export
exposición *f* exhibition
extintor *m* fire extinguisher
extranjero(a) *mf* foreigner

F

fábrica *f* factory
fácil easy
factura *f* receipt; bill; account
facturación *f* check-in
falda *f* skirt
falso(a) fake; false
farmacia *f* chemist's; pharmacy
farmacia de guardia duty chemist
faro *m* headlamp; lighthouse
faro antiniebla fog-lamp
favor *m* favour
por favor please
favorito(a) favourite
febrero *m* February
fecha *f* date
fecha de caducidad expiry date
feliz happy
femenino(a) feminine
feo(a) ugly
feria *f* trade fair; unfair
ferrocarril *m* railway
festivos *mpl* public holidays
fiebre *f* fever
fiesta *f* party; public holiday
fila *f* row; line *(queue)*
filete *m* fillet; steak
fin *m* end
fin de semana weekend
firma *f* signature
firmar to sign
firme aquí sign here
floristería *f* florist's shop
fontanero *m* plumber
foto *f* picture; photo
fotocopia *f* photocopy
fotografía *f* photograph
frágil fragile
francés(cesa) French

Francia *f* France
frecuente frequent
freír to fry
frenar to brake
freno *m* brake
frente a opposite
fresa *f* strawberry
fresco(a) fresh; crisp; cool
frío(a) cold
frito(a) fried
fruta *f* fruit
fruta del tiempo fruit in season
frutería *f* fruit shop
fuera outdoors; out
fuerte strong; loud
fumadores *mpl* smokers
fumar to smoke
prohibido fumar no smoking
función *f* show
funcionar to work, to function
no funciona out of order

G

gafas *fpl* glasses
gafas de sol sunglasses
galería *f* gallery
galería de arte art gallery
galés(lesa) Welsh
Gales *m* Wales
gallego(a) Galician
galleta *f* biscuit
ganar to earn; to win (*sports, etc*)
garantía *f* guarantee
garganta *f* throat
gas *m* gas
con gas fizzy, sparkling
sin gas non-fizzy; still
gaseosa *f* lemonade
gasoil *m* diesel
gasolina *f* petrol
gasolina sin plomo unleaded petrol
gasolinera *f* petrol station
gastar to spend (*money*)
gastos *mpl* expenses
gato *m* cat; jack (*for car*)
gente *f* people
girar to turn around
glorieta *f* roundabout
goma *f* rubber; eraser
gordo(a) fat
gótico(a) Gothic
gracias thank you
muchas gracias thank you very much
gramo *m* gram(me)
Gran Bretaña *f* Great Britain
grande large; big; tall

grandes almacenes *mpl* department store
gratis free *(costing nothing)*
grave serious *(accident, etc)*
gripe *f* flu
gris grey
grupo *m* group; band *(rock)*
grupo sanguíneo blood group
guantes *mpl* gloves
guapo(a) handsome; attractive
guardar to put away; to keep
guardia *f* guard
Guardia Civil Civil Guard
guía (telefónica) *f* phone directory
guitarra *f* guitar
gustar to like; to enjoy

H

habitación *f* room
habitación doble double room
habitación individual single room
hablar (con) to speak/talk to
se habla inglés English spoken
hacer to do; to make
hacer cola to queue
hacer turismo to sightsee
hacia toward(s)
hacia arriba upwards, up
hacia abajo downwards, down
hacia adelante forwards
hacia atrás backwards
hasta until; till
hay there is/ there are
hecho(a) finished; done
hecho a mano handmade
heladería *f* ice-cream parlour
helado *m* ice cream
hemorragia *f* haemorrhage
herida *f* wound; injury
hermano(a) *mf* brother/sister
hervido(a) boiled
hervir to boil
hielo *m* ice
con/sin hielo with/without ice
hígado *m* liver
hijo(a) *mf* son/daughter
hinchado(a) swollen
hipermercado *m* hypermarket
histórico(a) historic

hombre *m* man
hombro *m* shoulder
hora *f* hour; appointment; time
horario *m* timetable
horchata (de chufa) *f* refreshing tiger nut drink
horno *m* oven
al horno baked; roasted
hospital *m* hospital
hostal *m* small hotel; hostel
hotel *m* hotel
hoy today
huelga *f* strike *(of workers)*
hueso *m* bone
huésped *mf* guest
huevo *m* egg
humo *m* smoke

I

ida *f* outward journey
de ida y vuelta return *(ticket)*
idioma *m* language
iglesia *f* church
importar to matter; to import *(goods)*
importe total *m* total *(amount)*
imprescindible essential
impreso *m* form
impuesto *m* tax
incluido(a) included
inconsciente unconscious
individual individual; single
infarto *m* heart attack
infección *f* infection
inferior inferior; lower
inflamación *f* inflammation
informe *m* report *(medical, police)*
infracción *f* offence
infracción de tráfico traffic offence
Inglaterra *f* England
inglés(lesa) English
insecto *m* insect
insolación *f* sunstroke
instrucciones *fpl* directions; instructions
interesante interesting
interior inside
intermitente *m* indicator *(in car)*
interruptor *m* switch
invierno *m* winter
invitación *f* invitation
invitado(a) *mf* guest
invitar to invite
inyección *f* injection
ir to go

ir a buscar to fetch
irse a casa to go home
irse de to leave *(a place)*
Irlanda *f* Ireland
Irlanda del Norte *f* Northern Ireland
irlandés(desa) Irish
isla *f* island
Italia *f* Italy
italiano(a) Italian
itinerario *m* route; schedule
IVA *m* VAT
izq./izqda. *abbrev. for* **izquierda**
izquierda *f* left

J

jabón *m* soap
jamás never
jamón *m* ham
jamón serrano cured ham
jamón (de) York cooked ham
jardín *m* garden
jefe(a) *mf* chief; head; boss
joven young
joya *f* jewel
joyas jewellery
joyería *f* jeweller's
judías *fpl* beans
judías verdes green beans
jueves *m* Thursday
jugar to play; gamble
julio *m* July
juguete *m* toy
juguetería *f* toy shop
junio *m* June
junto(a) together
junto a next to
juventud *f* youth

K

kilo *m* kilo(gram)
kilometraje *m* mileage
kilometraje (i)limitado (un)limited mileage
kilómetro *m* kilometre
kiosko (de prensa) *m* newsstand
kleenex® *m* tissue

L

la the; her; it; you *(formal)*
labio *m* lip
laborable working *(day)*
laborables weekdays
lado *m* side
al lado de beside
ladrón(ona) *mf* thief
lago *m* lake
lámpara *f* lamp
lana *f* wool
lápiz *m* pencil

largo(a)	long
largo recorrido	long-distance *(train, etc)*
lata *f*	can *(container)*; tin
lavabo *m*	lavatory; washbasin
lavado(a)	washed
lavadora *f*	washing machine
lavar	to wash
lavarse	to wash oneself
leche *f*	milk
leche desnatada	skimmed milk
leche entera	wholemilk
leche semi-desnatada	semi-skimmed milk
lechuga *f*	lettuce
leer	to read
lejos	far
lengua *f*	language; tongue
lente *f*	lens
lentes de contacto	contact lenses
lentejas *fpl*	lentils
lentillas *fpl*	contact lenses
lento(a)	slow
letra *f*	letter *(of alphabet)*
levantar	to lift
levantarse	to get up; to rise
ley *f*	law
libra *f*	pound *(currency, weight)*
libra esterlina	pound sterling
libre	free/vacant
libre de impuestos	tax-free
librería *f*	bookshop
libro *m*	book
licencia *f*	permit; licence
licor *m*	liqueur
licores	spirits
límite *m*	limit; boundary
límite de velocidad	speed limit
limón *m*	lemon
limonada *f*	lemonade
limpiar	to clean
limpieza en seco *f*	dry-cleaning
limpio(a)	clean
linterna *f*	torch; flashlight
liso(a)	plain; smooth
listo(a)	ready
litro *m*	litre
llamada *f*	call
llamar	to call; to ring; to knock *(on door)*
llave *f*	key; tap; spanner
llaves del coche	car keys

Spanish – English

llegada *f* arrival
llegar to arrive; to come
llenar to fill; to fill in
lleno(a) full (up)
llevar to bring; to wear; to carry
lluvia *f* rain
local *m* premises; bar
lugar *m* place
lugar de nacimiento place of birth
lujo *m* luxury
luna *f* moon
luna de miel honeymoon
lunes *m* Monday
luz *f* light

M

macedonia *f* fruit salad
madera *f* wood
madre *f* mother
maduro(a) ripe; mature
mal/malo(a) bad *(weather, news)*
maleta *f* case; suitcase
maletero *m* boot *(car)*
mañana tomorrow
mañana *f* morning
mancha *f* stain; mark
mando a distancia *m* remote control
manera *f* way; manner
mano *f* hand
de segunda mano secondhand
maquinilla de afeitar shaver
manta *f* blanket
mantener to maintain; to keep
mantequilla *f* butter
manzana *f* apple; block *(of houses)*
manzanilla *f* camomile tea; dry sherry
mapa *m* map
mapa de carreteras road map
maquillaje *m* make-up
máquina *f* machine
máquina de afeitar razor
máquina de fotos camera
mar *m* sea
marcapasos *m* pacemaker
marcha *f* gear
marcha atrás reverse gear
marea *f* tide
marea alta/baja high/low tide
mareado(a) sick *(car, sea)*; dizzy

margarina *f* margarine
marido *m* husband
marisco *m* seafood; shellfish
marisquería *f* seafood restaurant
mármol *m* marble
marrón brown
marroquinería *f* leather goods
martes *m* Tuesday
marzo *m* March
más more; plus
más que more than
más tarde later
masculino(a) male
matar to kill
matrícula *f* number plate
matrimonio *m* marriage
mayo *m* May
mayor bigger; biggest
mayor de edad adult
mayores de 18 años over-18s
mechero *m* lighter
medianoche *f* midnight
medias *tfpl* tights; stockings
medicina *f* medicine; drug
médico(a) *mf* doctor
medida *f* measurement; size
medio *m* the middle
medio(a) half
media hora half an hour
media pensión half board
mediodía: midday; noon
Mediterráneo *m* Mediterranean
mejor best; better
mejor que better than
melocotón *m* peach
melón *m* melon
menor smaller/ smallest; least
menos minus; less; except
menos que less than
mensaje *m* message
mensual monthly
menú *m* menu
menú del día set menu
mercado *m* market
mercadillo flea market
mermelada *f* jam
mes *m* month
mesa *f* table
metro *m* metre; underground; tape measure
mi my
mí me
miel *f* honey
mientras while

Spanish – English

miércoles *m* Wednesday
mil thousand
milímetro *m* millimetre
minusválido(a) *mf* disabled person
mirar to look at; to watch
misa *f* mass *(in church)*
mismo(a) same
mitad *f* half
mochila *f* backpack; rucksack
moda *f* fashion
modo *m* way; manner
modo de empleo instructions for use
mojado(a) wet
moneda *f* currency; coin
introduzca monedas insert coins
monitor(a) de esquí *mf* ski instructor
montaña *f* mountain
montañismo *m* mountaineering
montar to ride
montar a caballo to horse ride
mordedura *f* bite
morder to bite
mostrador *m* counter; desk
mostrar to show
moto(cicleta) *f* (motor)bike
moto acuática jet ski
móvil *m* mobile phone
media pensión (MP) half board
mucho a lot; much
mucho(a) a lot (of); much
muchos(as) many
muela *f* tooth
muestra *f* exhibition;
mujer *f* woman; wife
multa *f* fine *(to be paid)*
mundo *m* world
muñeca *f* wrist; doll
museo *m* museum; art gallery
muy very
muy hecho(a) well done *(steak)*

N

nacional national; domestic *(flight)*
nacionalidad *f* nationality
nada nothing
de nada don't mention it
nada más nothing else
nadar to swim
nadie nobody
naranja *f* orange
nariz *f* nose

natación *f* swimming
natural natural; fresh; plain
Navidad *f* Christmas
necesario(a) necessary
necesitar to need; to require
negarse to refuse
negocios *mpl* business
negro(a) black
neumático *m* tyre
nevar to snow
nevera *f* refrigerator
niebla *f* fog
nieto(a) *mf* grandson/ daughter
nieve *f* snow
niña *f* girl; baby girl
ningún/ ninguno(a) none
niño *m* boy; baby; child
niños children *(infants)*
nivel *m* level; standard
Nº *abbrev. for* **número**
noche *f* night
esta noche tonight
Nochebuena *f* Christmas Eve
Nochevieja *f* New Year's Eve
nombre *m* name
norte *m* north
Norteamérica *f* America; USA
norte-americano(a) American
nosotros(as) we
noticias *tfpl* news
novia *f* girlfriend; fiancée; bride
noviembre *m* November
novio *m* boyfriend; fiancé; bridegroom
nublado(a) cloudy
nuestro(a) our; ours
Nueva Zelanda *f* New Zealand
nuevo(a) new
número *m* number; size; issue
número de móvil mobile mumber
nunca never

O

o or
o... o... either... or...
objetivo *m* lens *(on camera)*
objeto *m* object
objetos de valor valuables
obligatorio(a) compulsory
obra *f* work; play *(theatre)*
obtener to get *(to obtain)*

océano *m* ocean
octubre *m* October
ocupado engaged
oeste *m* west
oferta *f* special offer
oficina *f* office
oficina de Correos Post Office
ofrecer to offer
oído *m* ear
oír to hear
ojo *m* eye
olor *m* smell
operación *f* operation
oportunidades *tfpl* bargains
orden *f* command
orden *m* order
ordenador *m* computer
ordenador portátil laptop
ordenador de bolsillo palmtop, PDA
oreja *f* ear
organizar to arrange; to organize
oro *m* gold
oscuro(a) dark; dim
oso *m* bear *(animal)*
otoño *m* autumn; fall
otro(a) other; another
otra vez again

P

paciente *mf* patient *(in hospital)*
padre *m* father
padres parents
paella *f* paella *(rice dish)*
pagado(a) paid
pagar to pay for; to pay
pagar al contado to pay cash
página *f* page
página web website
Páginas Amarillas *fpl* Yellow Pages
pago *m* payment
país *m* country
paisaje *m* landscape; countryside
palabra *f* word
palacio *m* palace
pálido(a) pale
palo *m* stick; mast
palo de golf golf club
pan *m* bread; loaf of bread
panadería *f* bakery
panecillo *m* bread roll
pantalones *mpl* trousers

pantalones cortos	shorts
pantys *mpl*	tights
pañuelo *m*	handkerchief; scarf
pañuelo de papel	tissue
papel *m*	paper
papel higiénico	toilet paper
papelería *f*	stationer's
paquete *m*	packet; parcel
par	even *(number)*
par *m*	pair
para	for; towards
parabrisas *m*	windscreen
parachoques *m*	bumper *(car)*
parada *f*	stop
parado(a)	unemployed
parador *m*	state-run hotel
paraguas *m*	umbrella
parar	to stop
pareja *f*	couple *(2 people)*
parque *m*	park
parque de atracciones	funfair
parquímetro *m*	parking meter
parrilla *f*	grill; barbecue
a la parrilla	grilled
particular	private
partido *m*	match *(sport)*; party *(political)*
partir	to depart
pasaje *m*	ticket; fare; alleyway
pasajero(a) *mf*	passenger
pasaporte *m*	passport
pasar	to happen
pasatiempo *m*	hobby; pastime
Pascua *f*	Easter
¡Felices Pascuas!	Happy Easter!
paseo *m*	walk; avenue; promenade
pasillo *m*	corridor; aisle
paso *m*	step; pace
paso a nivel	level crossing
paso de peatones	pedestrian crossing
paso subterráneo	pedestrian underpass
pasta *f*	pastry; pasta
pasta de dientes	toothpaste
pastel *m*	cake; pie
pasteles	pastries
pastelería *f*	cakes and pastries; cake shop
patata *f*	potato
patatas fritas	french fries; crisps
peaje *m*	toll

Spanish – English

peatón(ona) *mf* pedestrian
pecho *m* chest; breast
pechuga *f* breast *(poultry)*
pedir to ask for; to order
pedir prestado to borrow
pegar to stick (on); to hit
peine *m* comb
pelar to peel *(fruit)*
película *f* film
peligro *m* danger
peligro de incendio fire hazard
peligroso(a) dangerous
pelo *m* hair
pelota *f* ball
pelota de golf golf ball
pelota de tenis tennis ball
peluquería *f* hairdresser's
pendientes *mpl* earrings

pensar to think
pensión *f* guesthouse
pensionista *mf* senior citizen
peor worse; worst
pequeño(a) little; small; tiny
pera *f* pear
perder to lose; to miss *(train, etc)*
perdido(a) missing *(lost)*
perdón *m* pardon; sorry
perdonar to forgive
perfumería *f* perfume shop
periódico *m* newspaper
permitido(a) permitted; allowed
permitir to allow; to let
pero but
perro *m* dog
persona *f* person
pesado(a) heavy; boring
pesar to weigh

pesca *f* fishing
pescadería *f* fishmonger's
pescado *m* fish
peso *m* weight; scales
pez *m* fish
picado(a) chopped; minced; rough *(sea)*; stung *(by insect)*
picadura *f* insect bite; sting
picante peppery; hot; spicy
picar to itch; to sting
pie *m* foot
piel *f* fur; skin; leather
pierna *f* leg
pieza *f* part; room
pijama *m* pyjamas
pila *f* battery *(radio, etc)*
píldora *f* pill
pimienta *f* pepper *(spice)*

pimiento *m* pepper *(vegetable)*
piña *f* pineapple
pinchar to have a puncture
pinchazo *m* puncture
pintura *f* paint; painting
Pirineos *mpl* Pyrenees
pisar to step on; to tread on
no pisar el césped keep off the grass
piscina *f* swimming pool
piso *m* floor; storey; flat
pista *f* track; court
plancha *f* iron *(for clothes)*
a la plancha grilled
planchar to iron
plano *m* plan; town map
planta *f* plant; floor; sole *(of foot)*
planta baja/alta ground/top floor
plata *f* silver
plátano *m* banana; plane tree
plato *m* plate; dish *(food)*; course
plato del día dish of the day
playa *f* beach; seaside
plaza *f* square *(in town)*
plaza de toros bull ring
plazas libres vacancies
pobre poor
poco(a) little
poco hecho(a) rare *(steak)*
pocos(as) (a) few
un poco de a bit of
poder to be able
policía *f* police
Policía Municipal/Local local police
Policía Nacional national police
polideportivo *m* leisure centre
pollo *m* chicken
polo *m* ice lolly; polo shirt
pomada *f* ointment
pomelo *m* grapefruit
poner to put
poner en marcha to start *(car)*
ponerse en contacto to contact
por by; per; through; about
por adelantado in advance
por correo by mail
por ejemplo for example

Spanish – English

porque because
portaequipajes *m* luggage rack
portero *m* caretaker; doorman
posible possible
postal *f* postcard
postre *m* dessert; pudding
potable drinkable
precio *m* price; cost
precioso(a) lovely
preferir to prefer
prefijo *m* dialling code
pregunta *f* question
preguntar to ask
preocupado(a) worried
preparar to prepare; to cook
presentar to introduce
preservativo *m* condom

presión *f* pressure
presión arterial blood pressure
prestar to lend
primavera *f* spring *(season)*
primer/o(a) first
primeros auxilios *mpl* first aid
principal main
principiante *mf* beginner
prioridad (de paso) *f* right of way
privado(a) private
probador *m* changing room
probar to try; to taste
probarse to try on *(clothes)*
procedente de... coming from...
productos *mpl* produce; products
productos lácteos dairy products
profundo(a) deep

programa *m* programme
prohibido(a) prohibited/no...
prohibido aparcar/estacionar no parking
prohibido bañarse no bathing
prohibido el paso no entry
pronto soon
pronunciar to pronounce
propiedad *f* property
propietario(a) *mf* owner
propina *f* tip
propio(a) own
protector solar *m* suncream
próximo(a) next
pueblo *m* village; country
puente *m* bridge

puerta *f* door; gate
cierren la puerta close the door
puerta de embarque boarding gate
puerto *m* port
puesto de socorro first-aid post
puesto que since
pulpo *m* octopus
pulsera *f* bracelet
puro *m* cigar

Q

que than; that; which
¿qué? what?; which?
¿qué tal? how are you?
quedar to remain; to be left
quedar bien to fit *(clothes)*
queja *f* complaint
quemado(a) burnt
quemadura *f* burn
quemar to burn
querer to want; to love
querer decir to mean
queso *m* cheese
¿quién? who?
quiosco *m* kiosk
quitar to remove
quizá(s) perhaps

R

ración *f* portion
raciones portions
radio *m* spoke *(wheel)*
radiografía *f* X-ray
rápido *m* express train
rápido(a) quick; fast
raqueta *f* racket
rato *m* a while
raton *m* mouse
razón *f* reason
real royal
rebajas *tfpl* sale(s)
recambio *m* spare; refill
recargar to recharge *(battery, etc)*
recibir to receive
recibo *m* receipt
recientemente recently
reclamación *f* claim; complaint
reclamar to claim
recoger to collect
recogida de equipajes baggage reclaim
recomendar to recommend
recuerdo *m* souvenir
reembolsar to reimburse; to refund
reembolso *m* refund

Spanish - English

refresco *m* refreshment; cold drink
regalo *m* gift; present
régimen *m* diet
región *f* district; area; region
registrarse to register *(at hotel)*
regla *f* period *(menstruation)*; ruler *(for measuring)*
Reino Unido *m* United Kingdom
reírse to laugh
rellenar to fill in
reloj *m* clock; watch
RENFE *f* Spanish National Railways
reparación *f* repair
reparar to repair
repetir to repeat
reproductor de CD/DVD *m* CD/DVD player
reproductor MP3 *m* MP3 player
repuestos *mpl* spare parts
reserva *f* booking(s); reservation
reservado(a) reserved
reservar to reserve; to book
resfriado *m* cold *(illness)*
respirar to breathe
responder to answer; to reply
respuesta *f* answer
resto *m* the rest
retrasado(a) delayed
retraso *m* delay
sin retraso on schedule
reunión *f* meeting
revelar to develop *(photos)*
revista *f* magazine
riñón *m* kidney
río *m* river
robar to steal
robo *m* robbery; theft
rodilla *f* knee
rojo(a) red
románico(a) Romanesque
romper to break; to tear
ropa *f* clothes
rosa *f* rose
rosa pink
rosado *m* rosé
roto(a) broken
rotonda *f* roundabout *(traffic)*

rubio(a) blond; fair haired
rueda *f* wheel
rueda de repuesto spare tyre
rueda pinchada flat tyre
ruido *m* noise
ruta *f* route
ruta turística tourist route

S

sábado *m* Saturday
sábana *f* sheet *(bed)*
saber to know *(facts)*; to know how *(to do something)*
sacar to take out *(of bag, etc)*
sacarina *f* saccharin
sal *f* salt
sin sal unsalted
sala *f* hall; hospital ward
salado(a) savoury; salty
salchicha *f* sausage
saldos *mpl* sales
salida *f* exit/departure
salir to go out; to come out
salmón *m* salmon
salsa *f* gravy; sauce; dressing
saltar to jump
salteado(a) sauté; sautéed
salud *f* health
sandalias *tfpl* sandals
sandía *f* watermelon
sangrar to bleed
secar to dry
seco(a) dry; dried *(fruit, beans)*
seguida:
en seguida straight away
seguido(a) continuous
seguir to continue; to follow
según according to
segundo *m* second *(time)*
segundo(a) second
seguramente probably, almost certainly
seguridad *f* reliability; safety; security
seguro *m* insurance
seguro del coche car insurance
seguro de vida life insurance
sello *m* stamp *(postage)*
semáforo *m* traffic lights
semana *f* week
semanal weekly

Spanish – English

señal *f* sign; signal; road sign
sencillo(a) simple; single *(ticket)*
señor *m* gentleman
Señor (Sr.) Mr; Sir
señora *f* lady
Señora (Sra.) Mrs; Ms; Madam
señoras ladies
señorita *f* Miss
Señorita (Srta.)... Miss...
sentarse to sit
sentir to feel
separado(a) separated
septiembre *m* September
ser to be
servicio *m* service; service charge
área de servicios service area

servicio incluido service included
servicios toilets
servilleta *f* serviette
servir to serve
seta *f* mushroom
sexo *m* sex; gender
si if
sí yes
sida *m* AIDS
sidra *f* cider
siempre always
siento:
lo siento I'm sorry
siga follow
siga adelante carry on
siga recto keep straight on
siguiente following; next
silla *f* chair; seat
silla de ruedas wheelchair
sillón *m* armchair

simpático(a) nice; kind
sin without
sin plomo unleaded
sírvase vd./ud. mismo self-service/help yourself
sitio *m* place; space; position; site
sobre on; upon; about; on top of
sobrio(a) sober
sociedad *f* society, company *(business)*
Sociedad Anónima Ltd; plc
socio(a) *mf* member; partner *(business)*
¡socorro! help!
sol *m* sun; sunshine
solamente only

solicitar to request
solo(a) alone; lonely
sólo only
solomillo *m* sirloin steak
soltero(a) *mf* bachelor/ spinster
soltero(a) single *(unmarried)*
sombra *f* shade; shadow
sombrero *m* hat
sombrilla *f* sunshade; parasol
sonido *m* sound
sonreír to smile
sonrisa *f* smile
sopa *f* soup
sordo(a) deaf
Sr. *abbrev. for* **señor**
Sra. *abbrev. for* **señora**
Srta. *abbrev. for* **señorita**
stop *m* stop *(sign)*
su his/her/its/ their/your
suavizante *m* hair conditioner; fabric softener
submarinismo *m* scuba diving
sucio(a) dirty
sucursal *f* branch *(of bank, etc)*
suelo *m* soil; ground; floor
suelto *m* small change
suerte *f* luck
¡(buena) suerte! good luck!
sujetador *m* bra
supermercado *m* supermarket
sur *m* south
surfing *m* surfing
surtidor *m* petrol pump
sus his/her/their/ your

T

tabaco *m* tobacco; cigarettes
tablao (flamenco) *m* Flamenco show
TALGO *m* Intercity express train
talla *f* size
taller *m* garage *(for repairs)*
también as well; also; too
tampoco neither
tampones *mpl* tampons
taquilla *f* ticket office
tarde *f* evening; afternoon
tarde late

Spanish - English

tarjeta *f* card
tarjeta de crédito credit card
tarjéta de débito debit card
tarjeta de embarque boarding pass
tasca *f* bar; cheap restaurant
taxista *mf* taxi driver
taza *f* cup
té *m* tea
teatro *m* theatre
telefonear to phone
teléfono *m* phone
teléfono público payphone
telesilla *m* ski lift; chairlift
televisión *f* television
temporada *f* season
temporada alta/baja high/low season

tenedor *m* fork *(for eating)*
tener to have
tener fiebre to have a temperature
ternera *f* veal
terraza *f* terrace; balcony
tiempo *m* time; weather
tienda *f* store; shop; tent
tienda de ropa clothes shop
tijeras *tfpl* scissors
timbre *m* doorbell; official stamp
tintorería *f* dry-cleaner's
tío *m* uncle
típico(a) typical
tipo *m* sort
tipo de cambio exchange rate
tirar to throw (away); to pull
para tirar disposable
tire pull

tirita *f* (sticking) plaster
toalla *f* towel
tobillo *m* ankle
tocar to touch; to play *(instrument)*
todo(a) all
todo everything
todo incluido all inclusive
tomar to take; to have *(food/drink)*
tomar el sol to sunbathe
tomate *m* tomato
tónica *f* tonic water
tonto(a) stupid
torcedura *f* sprain
torero *m* bullfighter
tormenta *f* thunderstorm
toro *m* bull
torre *f* tower
tos *f* cough

escape *m*

tostada *f* toast
trabajar to work *(person)*
trabajo *m* work
traducción *f* translation
traer to fetch; to bring
traje *m* suit; outfit
traje de baño swimsuit
tranquilo(a) calm; quiet
transbordo *m* transfer
tranvía *m* tram; short-distance train
travesía *f* crossing
tren *m* train
trozo *m* piece
tú you *(singular with friends)*
tu your *(singular with friends)*
tumbona *f* deckchair
túnel *m* tunnel
turista *mf* tourist

U

Ud(s). *abbrev. for* **usted(es)**
últimamente lately
último(a) last
un(a) a/an
uña *f* nail *(finger, toe)*
únicamente only
Unión Europea *f* European Union
universidad *f* university
unos(as) some
urgencias *tfpl* A&E, casualty department
urgente urgent; express
usted you *(polite singular)*
ustedes you *(polite plural)*
útil useful
utilizar to use
uva *f* grape

V

vacaciones *tfpl* holiday
vacío(a) empty
vacuna *f* vaccination
vagón *m* railway carriage
vale OK
válido(a) valid *(ticket, licence, etc)*
vapor *m* steam
al vapor steamed
vaqueros *mpl* jeans
variado(a) assorted; mixed

Spanish – English

varios(as)	several
vasco(a)	Basque
vaso *m*	glass *(for drinking)*
veces *tfpl*	times
vecino(a) *mf*	neighbour
vehículo *m*	vehicle
velocidad *f*	speed
límite de velocidad	speed limit
velocidad máxima	speed limit
venda *f*	bandage
vendedor(a) *m/f*	salesman/woman
vender	to sell
se vende	for sale
venir	to come
venta *f*	sale; country inn
ventilador *m*	fan *(electric)*
ver	to see; to watch
verano *m*	summer
verdad *f*	truth
¿de verdad?	really?
verde	green
verduras *tfpl*	vegetables
vestido *m*	dress
vestirse	to get dressed
veterinario(a) *mf*	vet
vez *f*	time
viajar	to travel
viaje *m*	journey; trip
viaje de negocios	business trip
viajero *m*	traveller
vida *f*	life
viejo(a)	old
viento *m*	wind
viernes *m*	Friday
vinagre *m*	vinegar
vino *m*	wine
violación *f*	rape
violar	to rape
virus *m*	virus
visita *f*	visit
viudo(a) *m/f*	widow/widower
vivir	to live
V.O. (versión original)	undubbed version (of film)
volar	to fly
volver	to come/go back; to return
vosotros	you *(plural with friends)*
vuelo *m*	flight
vuestro(a)	your *(plural with friends)*

wáter *m* lavatory; toilet

Y

y and
yo I; me
yogur *m* yoghurt

Z

zanahoria *f* carrot
zapatería *f* shoe shop
zapato *m* shoe
zumo *m* juice

Collins Easy: Photo Phrasebook

Also available as
**Phrasebook
CD Pack**

**Other titles
in the series**
Easy French
Easy Greek
Easy Italian